Campbell's™

EASY HOME COOKING

One-Dish Chicken & Stuffing Bake (page 33)

Campbell's™

EASY HOME COOKING

WILTON HOUSE

Published by Joshua Morris Publishing, Inc.
355 Riverside Avenue
Westport, CT 06880

Photography: Dennis Gottlieb.
Prop styling: Randi Barrett.
Food styling: Mariann Sauvion, Rick Ellis.
Foodstylist assistants: Chris Fost, Brett Kurzweil.
Grateful acknowledgement is made for tableware props provided by Sasaki, Cassis & Co. and Ann Mallory.

Designed by Jane Wilson.

Campbell's Easy Home Cooking was produced by the Global Publishing division of Campbell Soup Company, Campbell Place, Camden, NJ 08103-1799.

Senior Managing Editor:	Pat Teberg
Assistant Editors:	Peg Romano, Ginny Gance, Joanne Fullan
Global Consumer Food Center:	Jane Freiman, Ann Dungan, Nancy Speth, Sue Lawrence
Marketing Manager:	Michael Conway
Public Relations Manager:	Mary Beth Kramer

Pictured on the front cover: One-Dish Chicken & Stuffing Bake (page 33).
Pictured on the back cover: Clockwise from top right: Easy Chicken & Pasta (page 48), Spicy Vegetable Chili (page 126), Chicken Enchiladas (page 42).

Preparation and Cooking Times: Every recipe was developed and tested in Campbell's Global Consumer Food Center by professional home economists. Use "Chill Time," "Cook Time," "Cool Time," "Marinating Time," "Prep Time" and/or "Stand Time" given with each recipe as guides. The preparation times are based on the approximate amount of time required to assemble the recipes *before* baking or cooking. These times include preparation steps, such as chopping; mixing; cooking rice, pasta, vegetables; etc. The fact that some preparation steps can be done simultaneously or during cooking is taken into account. The cook times are based on the minimum amount of time to cook, bake or broil the food in the recipes.

First Edition
10 9 8 7 6 5 4 3 2 1

Printed and bound in the United States of America.

ISBN: 0-88705-897-3

TABLE OF CONTENTS

Campbell's™

EASY HOME COOKING

Everyone is busy these days, and that means cooking on-the-run or, sometimes, no cooking at all. If you love to eat and eat well, there's no substitute for a great-tasting home-cooked meal. Now Campbell's shows you how to simplify mealtime preparation and create fabulous meals to serve your family and friends. *Campbell's Easy Home Cooking* offers over 125 delicious, kitchen-tested recipes and dozens of full color photographs. This book gives you all the ingredients to prepare delicious, no-fuss meals every night of the week.

Campbell's Family of Quality Products

*C*ooking with Campbell's is as easy as 1, 2, 3. Here we've illustrated some simple cooking techniques to help you take the guesswork out of recipe preparation and help you streamline your time and effort in the kitchen. You'll see the difference between chopping, cubing and mincing. You'll see how to measure ingredients the correct way. You'll see how to trim broccoli, quickly chop onion and more.

Chopping refers to cutting a food into irregular pieces about the size of peas, as shown here with celery.

To chop an onion quickly, trim ends and peel outer skin. Halve onion from top to root end. Place the halves flat side down; make parallel vertical slices. Then cut across the slices, as shown. This works well for other vegetables, too, such as potatoes.

Cubing refers to cutting a food into uniform pieces. Cut foods into strips about $\frac{1}{2}$ inch wide. Line up strips, then cut crosswise into $\frac{1}{2}$- inch pieces, shown here with ham.

To mince fresh garlic, use a utility knife to cut peeled cloves into very tiny, irregular pieces.

To crush garlic, place a peeled clove in a garlic press and clamp the handles together.

To thinly slice green onions, trim root ends. Strip off and discard wilted outer leaves. Line up two or three green onions and with a small sharp utility knife, cut into thinly sliced pieces.

To easily slice beef for stir-frying, place beef in freezer up to 1 hour or until firm. Slice beef across the grain into thin strips.

To measure liquids, use a glass or clear plastic liquid measuring cup placed on a level surface. Bend down so your eye is level with the marking on the cup.

Shredding means to cut a food into long, narrow strips, usually by rubbing it across a shredding surface. Use a finer shredding surface for short, very narrow strips. Use a shredder for cheese and vegetables. Some vegetables, such as lettuce or cabbage, can be shredded by thinly slicing with a knife.

Grating means to rub a food across a rough grating surface to make very fine particles. Grate hard cheeses such as Parmesan, potent seasonings such as gingerroot or whole spices such as nutmeg.

When handling and slicing fresh jalapeño peppers, wear rubber gloves to protect your hands from the burning oils of the peppers.

To trim fresh broccoli, remove large outer leaves and trim off tough parts and ends of stalks. For spears, cut lengthwise two or three times. For flowerets, cut top part of stalks into small clusters.

EQUIVALENT MEASUREMENTS

MEASURE	EQUIVALENT		MEASURE	EQUIVALENT
Teaspoons			**Cups**	
Under 1/8 teaspoon	Dash		1/8 cup	1 ounce = 2 tablespoons
3 teaspoons	1 tablespoon		1/4 cup	2 ounces = 4 tablespoons
			1/3 cup	5 tablespoons plus 1 teaspoon
Tablespoons			1/2 cup	4 ounces = 8 tablespoons
1 tablespoon	3 teaspoons		3/4 cup	6 ounces = 12 tablespoons
4 tablespoons	1/4 cup = 2 ounces		1 cup	8 ounces = 16 tablespoons
5 1/3 tablespoons	1/3 cup			= 1/2 pint
8 tablespoons	1/2 cup = 4 ounces		2 cups	16 ounces = 1 pint
10 2/3 tablespoons	2/3 cup		4 cups	32 ounces = 1 quart
12 tablespoons	3/4 cup = 6 ounces		8 cups	64 ounces = 2 quarts
16 tablespoons	1 cup = 8 ounces			= 1/2 gallon
			16 cups	128 ounces = 4 quarts
Useful Equivalents				= 1 gallon
1 pound	16 ounces			
1 liter	1.06 quarts			

COMMON FOOD EQUIVALENTS

Apples, 1 medium	about 1 cup sliced		Macaroni, elbow, 8 oz. dry	about 4 cups cooked
Bananas, 1 lb.	3 medium or 1 1/3 cups mashed		Margarine or butter	
			1 lb.	4 sticks or 2 cups
Bread, 1-lb. loaf	14 to 20 slices		1/4 lb. stick	1/2 cup or 8 tbsp.
Bread crumbs, dried 8 oz.	2 1/4 cups		Meat, 1 lb. boneless cooked	3 cups diced
Bread crumbs, 2 slices			Meat, 1 lb. raw boneless	2 cups cooked, cubed
fresh bread	1 cup soft crumbs		Mushrooms, 1 lb.	about 6 cups sliced
Broccoli, 1 bunch (about 1lb.)	about 3 cups flowerets		Noodles, dry medium (3 cups)	about 3 cups cooked
Carrot, 1 medium	about 1/2 cup shredded		Onion, 1 large yellow	3/4 to 1 cup chopped
Cauliflower, 1 small head			Orange, 1 medium	1/3 to 1/2 cup juice
(about 1 1/2 lb.)	about 4 cups flowerets		Parmesan cheese, 4 oz.	1 1/4 cups grated
Celery, 1 stalk	about 1/2 cup sliced		Potatoes, 1 lb. all-purpose	3 medium or about
Cheddar cheese, 1lb.	4 cups shredded			3 1/2 cups chopped or
Cream cheese, 8 oz.	1 cup (16 tbsp.)			2 to 3 cups mashed
Cream,			Poultry, 1 lb. boneless, cooked	3 cups diced
heavy or whipping, 1 cup	2 cups whipped		Rice	
Egg, 1 large	3 tbsp. beaten egg		1 cup *uncooked* regular	
Flour, 1 lb. all-purpose	3 1/2 cups		long-grain	about 3 cups cooked
Green beans, 1 lb.,			1 cup *uncooked* quick-cooking	about 2 cups cooked
cut into 1-inch pieces	about 3 cups		Spaghetti, 8 oz. dry	about 4 cups cooked
Green onion, 1 medium,			Sour cream, 8 oz.	1 cup
sliced	about 2 tbsp.		Sugar, 1 lb.	
Green pepper, 1 large	about 1 cup chopped		granulated	2 cups
Herbs, fresh, 1 tbsp. chopped	1 tsp. dried leaves		brown	2 1/4 cups packed
Lemon, 1 medium	about 3 tbsp. juice or		confectioners'	about 4 cups
	about 1 tbsp. grated		Swiss cheese, 1lb.	4 cups shredded
	peel		Tomatoes, 1lb.	3 medium

*F*ollow these guidelines for storing foods in the refrigerator, freezer or on the pantry shelf.

- Check expiration dates and use products within the recommended time.
- Arrange items in the refrigerator or freezer to allow air to circulate evenly.
- Use containers and wraps designed especially for maintaining freshness, textures and color of frozen foods such as plastic containers with tight-fitting lids, freezer paper and heavy-duty plastic bags.
- Refrigerate perishable items promptly after shopping.
- Hot foods should be cooled before refrigerating

to maintain a refrigerator temperature of 40°F.
- Pantry storage areas should be dark and dry and free of insects.
- It is recommended to use plastic containers with tight-fitting lids to store pantry foods after opening.
- Avoid storing cans with swollen ends or dents on pantry shelf.
- It is important to check to see if pantry foods should be refrigerated after opening. (Times given in Pantry Storage are for *unopened* food items.)

*T*hese storage time limits will help keep refrigerated foods from spoiling. The limits given for frozen and pantry foods are to maintain peak flavor and quality of foods. However, successful storage depends on such factors as type of refrigerator/freezer, how often it is opened and quality of containers or packaging materials used. Try to use foods *before* stated storage time limits.

FOOD	REFRIGERATOR (40°F.)	FREEZER (0°F.)	PANTRY (50°F. to 70°F.)
Apples	1 month	—	—
Baking powder or soda	—	—	18 months
Butter	2 weeks	5 months	—
Eggs			
Fresh	3 weeks	Not recommended	—
Hard-cooked	1 week	Not recommended	—
Canned foods	—	—	1-2 years
Cheese			
ricotta	5 days	2 weeks	—
cream	2 weeks	Not recommended	—
whole pieces	2 months	—	—
Fish or shellfish	1 day	3-6 months	—

FOOD	REFRIGERATOR (40°F.)	FREEZER (0°F.)	PANTRY (50°F. to 70°F.)
Flour	—	—	2-3 months
Lemons	2 weeks	—	—
Macaroni or spaghetti (dry)	—	—	1 year
Margarine	1 month	1 year	—
Meats			
Bacon	7 days	1 month	—
Beef, roasts	3-5 days	6-12 months	—
Beef, steaks	3-5 days	6-12 months	—
Frankfurters	1 week	2 weeks	—
Ground beef, lamb, pork or poultry	1-2 days	3-4 months	—
Ham, canned, labeled "keep refrigerated"	6-9 months	Not recommended	—
Ham, fully cooked slices	3-4 days	1-2 months	—
Lamb chops	3-5 days	6-9 months	—
Pork chops	3-5 days	4-6 months	—
Pork, roasts	3-5 days	4-6 months	—
Sausage, raw beef, pork or poultry	1-2 days	1-2 months	—
Smoked breakfast links or patties	7 days	1-2 months	—
Stew meat beef, lamb or pork	1-2 days	3-4 months	—
Milk	1 week	—	—
Oil olive	—	—	1 month
vegetable	—	—	6-12 months
Oranges	2 weeks	—	—
Poultry			
Chicken or turkey, whole	1-2 days	1 year	—
Chicken or turkey pieces	1-2 days	6 months	—
Rice, white	—	—	2 years
Salad dressings	—	—	6 months
Sugar, granulated	—	—	2 years
brown or confectioners'	—	—	4 months
Vegetables (See Fresh Vegetable Guide, page 16)			
Vinegar	—	—	6 months

$\mathcal{H}$erbs and spices add flavor, aroma and color to recipes. Use these seasonings sparingly, as flavors increase as food cooks. Many of these seasonings make tasty sodium and sugar substitutes. Herbs are aromatic leaves while spices consist of the seeds, buds, fruit or flower parts, bark or roots of plants.

example, use 1 tablespoon chopped *fresh* basil for 1 teaspoon *dried* basil.

After measuring dried herb leaves, crush them before using to release their aromatic oils.

When using an unfamiliar herb, use about $1/4$ teaspoon dried herb (whole leaves) or $1/8$ teaspoon ground dried herb for 4 servings, then taste before adding more.

Frozen fresh herbs can be added to recipes while still frozen.

It is recommended to add herbs near the end of cooking time as the delicate herb flavors *do not* hold up well when cooked more than 30 minutes.

With a few exceptions, like cinnamon sticks, whole spices are easy to grind in a pepper mill or coffee grinder.

HOW TO STORE

For fresh herbs: Immerse freshly cut stems in water then cover loosely with a plastic bag. Store for a few days in refrigerator. Can also be frozen for up to 6 months.

Dried herbs and ground or whole spices should be stored in airtight containers in a cool, dry place away from heat and sunlight for up to 1 year.

Red spices (paprika, chili powder, etc.) retain their color and flavor if stored tightly sealed in the refrigerator.

HOW TO USE

Because dried herbs have a stronger flavor than fresh, substitute *three times* as much of a chopped fresh herb for the dried one when cooking. For

HERBS

BASIL
- Fragrant leaves with an aniselike flavor and sweet aroma.
- Available: fresh, dried leaves or ground.
- Use to flavor meats, poultry, soups, stews and vegetables. It is the main ingredient in pesto.

BAY LEAF
- Green, aromatic, shiny leaves with a pungent woodsy flavor.
- Available: fresh, dried whole leaves or ground. Remove leaf before serving and discard.
- Use to flavor meats, fish, soups, stews and vegetables.

CHIVES
- Long tubular leaves with a mild onion flavor.
- Available: fresh, freeze-dried or frozen.
- Use to flavor eggs, salads, sauces and vegetables.

CILANTRO (also known as Chinese parsley)

- Delicate dark green leaves with a pungent flavor.
- Available: fresh or dried leaves.
- Used in Chinese, Indian and Mexican cuisines and to flavor meats, poultry and sauces.

DILL

- Feathery green leaves with a delicate, distinctive flavor.
- Available: fresh or dried leaves (dried dill is known as dill weed) and seeds.
- Use to flavor fish, pickles, poultry, salads, savory baked goods, vegetables and vinegars.

MINT

- The two most popular varieties are peppermint and spearmint. Peppermint has a strong, sweet cool flavor. Spearmint has a mild sweet flavor.
- Available: fresh or dried leaves and in extract or oil forms.
- Use to flavor beverages, fruits, jellies, lamb, sauces and tomatoes.

OREGANO

- Small grayish-green leaves with a strong, pungent slightly bitter flavor.
- Available: fresh or dried leaves and ground.
- Use to flavor tomato-based sauces, pork, lamb, seafood and vegetables.

PARSLEY

- Dark green leaves with a mild peppery flavor. The two most popular forms of parsley are *curly leaf* or *flat leaf* (Italian).
- Available: fresh or dehydrated leaves called parsley flakes.
- Use as a garnish and to flavor any dish.

ROSEMARY

- Resembling small pine needles, the silver-green needle-shaped leaves are aromatic with a pungent, pine-like aroma and a bittersweet flavor.
- Available: fresh or dried leaves.
- Use to flavor dressings, lamb, poultry, stuffing and vegetables.

TARRAGON

- Aromatic, dark green leaves with a distinctive licorice-like flavor.
- Available: fresh or dried leaves.
- Use to flavor dressings, eggs, fish, salads, sauces and vinegars.

THYME

- Tiny, oval-shaped gray-green leaves with a spicy aroma and a strong, distinctive taste.
- Available: fresh or dried leaves and ground.
- Use to flavor cream sauces, fish, poultry, meat and soups.

SPICES

ALLSPICE

- Flavor resembles a blend of cinnamon, cloves and nutmeg.
- Available: smooth, brown whole berries or ground.
- Use to flavor desserts, beef, pork and tomato sauce.

CHILI POWDER

- A ground blend of mild chili peppers, oregano, cumin, garlic and sometimes salt. It has a hot spicy, peppery flavor.
- Available: ground.
- Use to flavor Mexican-style dishes, meats, poultry, eggs, fish, stews and vegetables.

CINNAMON

- A sweet and pungent spice is the dried bark of evergreen trees native to Southeast Asia.
- Available: ground or as reddish-brown sticks.
- Use to flavor fruits, desserts, breads and beverages.

CLOVES

- Dried, rich-brown, unopened flower buds of a tropical evergreen tree.
- Available: whole or ground.
- Use to flavor desserts, baked goods, beverages, lamb and tomato sauce.

GINGER

- The root of a tropical plant, it has a pungent, sweet aroma and a hot taste.
- Available: fresh (refrigerate and use within one week) and ground.
- Use to flavor fruits, poultry, pork and desserts.

NUTMEG

- Large oval wrinkled seeds of the nutmeg tree imparts a warm, sweet spicy flavor.
- Available: whole or ground.
- Use to flavor fruits, eggnog, cheese, desserts, beef, vegetables and many sauces.

PAPRIKA

- Made by grinding the pods of mild sweet chilies or peppers with flavor ranging from mild to hot.
- Available: ground and in color from bright red to brick-red. Store paprika in the refrigerator.
- Use as a garnish or to flavor fish and vegetables.

RED PEPPER

- Made from dried, ripe hot chili peppers with a hot and pungent flavor.
- Available: ground (cayenne) or small dark-red flakes.
- Use to flavor tomato sauces, vegetables, eggs, soups, dressings and sauces.

Use this handy guide for tips on selecting the best vegetables, basic preparation and storing hints to help ensure peak flavor and freshness.

VEGETABLE	BASIC PREPARATION	STORAGE
Asparagus - Select firm, brittle spears that are bright green almost the entire length, with tightly closed tips.	Rinse thoroughly to remove dirt and sand. Snap off and discard tough ends. If desired, gently peel stalks with a vegetable peeler to remove scales. Leave spears whole or cut into 1-inch pieces.	Wrap ends in a damp paper towel. Place *unwashed* asparagus in a perforated plastic bag and refrigerate for up to 4 days.
Beans (green or wax) - Choose small crisp beans that are bright and blemish-free.	Rinse thoroughly; snap off and discard ends. Leave whole or slice diagonally into 1-inch pieces or slice lengthwise (French-style).	Place *unwashed* beans in a perforated plastic bag and refrigerate for up to 4 days.
Broccoli - Look for firm stalks with compact clusters of tightly closed dark green flowerets. Avoid heads with yellowing flowerets and thick, woody stalks.	Rinse and cut off and discard ends of stalks, leaving about 3½ inches of stalks. Cut lengthwise into spears. Leave spears whole and slash through bottom inch of stalks or slice stalks into pieces. Cut top part of stalks into flowerets.	Place *unwashed* broccoli in a plastic bag and refrigerate for up to 5 days.
Cabbage - Choose firm heads that feel heavy for their size. Outer leaves should look fresh and be blemish-free.	Remove any wilted outer leaves. Rinse and cut into wedges or shred; discard core.	Place *unwashed* cabbage in a plastic bag and refrigerate for up to 2 weeks.
Carrots - Select firm carrots that are smooth, well-shaped and brightly colored. Any tops (leaves) should look fresh and be bright green.	Trim top and root ends. Peel with vegetable peeler to remove thin layer of skin and rinse. Cook whole or slice, dice, shred or cut into strips.	Place *unwashed* carrots in a plastic bag and refrigerate for up to 2 weeks.
Cauliflower - Choose firm, compact, creamy white heads. A yellow tinge and spreading flowerets indicate over-maturity. Any leaves should be crisp and bright green.	Remove outer leaves and cut out core; discard. Rinse head. Leave head whole or break into flowerets.	Place *unwashed* cauliflower in a plastic bag and refrigerate for up to 1 week.
Celery - Select rigid, crisp green stalks with fresh-looking leaves. Avoid celery with limp or rubbery stalks.	Separate stalks and rinse thoroughly. Trim off bottoms, leaves and any blemishes. Slice, chop or dice as needed.	Rinse and shake dry. Wrap in moist paper towels and place in plastic bag and refrigerate for up to 2 weeks.
Cucumber - Choose firm, dark green cucumbers that are well-shaped and slender. Soft, yellowing cucumbers are past their peak.	Rinse and, if desired, peel with a vegetable peeler or score lengthwise with tines of fork. To seed, cut cucumber in half lengthwise and scoop out seeds with a spoon.	Refrigerate whole cucumbers, *unwrapped*, for up to 2 weeks.
Garlic - Choose firm, dry bulbs with tightly closed cloves and smooth skins. Avoid bulbs with sprouting green shoots.	Break into cloves. To peel, cut off root end of clove, crush clove with side of knife blade and peel skin away. Mince or press through garlic press.	Store *unwrapped* garlic in a cool (50°F.), dry, dark place with good ventilation for up to 3 months.

VEGETABLE	BASIC PREPARATION	STORAGE
GREEN ONIONS (scallions) - Select green onions with bright green tops and clean, white roots.	Rinse and pat dry. Trim root ends and discard wilted outer leaves. Trim brown or dried areas from tops. Slice or cut into strips.	Place *unwashed* green onions in a plastic bag and refrigerate for up to 1 week.
LETTUCE - Choose heads of *iceberg* with fresh, green outer leaves. Heads should give a little under pressure. *Romaine* has crisp, deep green outer leaves without brown spots. *Bibb, Boston, butter, red or green leaf* should have tender, fresh-looking leaves free of tip burn and bruising.	Trim away wilted outer leaves and tough ribs. Tear leaves into bite-size pieces. Cut lettuce only when recipe calls for wedges or shredding.	Rinse before storing. To rinse iceberg, hold head, core side down, under cold running water. Rinse remaining varieties under running water, separating individual leaves. Dry. Wrap in paper towels and place in a plastic bag. Refrigerate iceberg and romaine for up to 5 days and the others for up to 2 days.
MUSHROOMS - Select smooth, plump mushrooms with caps closed around stems. Avoid spotted mushrooms and those that have open caps with dark gills exposed.	To clean, gently wipe with a damp cloth or mushroom brush, or rinse briefly under cold running water; gently pat dry. Trim stems. Use whole, slice or chop as recipe directs.	Place *unwashed* mushrooms in a paper bag and refrigerate for up to 4 days. Place a damp paper towel inside bag to retain moisture.
ONIONS (yellow) - Select firm, dry onions with brittle outer skin. Avoid those with sprouting green shoots and dark spots.	Trim ends and peel outer skin. Leave whole, quarter, slice or chop.	Store whole onions, *unwrapped*, in a cool (50°F.) dry, dark place with good ventilation for up to 2 months. Wrap cut pieces in plastic wrap and refrigerate for up to 4 days.
PEAS (green) - Select small, plump bright green pods that are firm, crisp and well-filled with medium-size peas.	Remove peas from pods and rinse.	Place *unwashed* pods in a plastic bag and refrigerate for up to 3 days.
PEPPERS (green or red) - Select bright, glossy peppers that are firm, well-shaped and without bruises. Avoid those with soft spots or gashes.	Rinse and remove stem, seeds and white membrane. Leave whole, cut in half lengthwise, slice, dice or cut into strips or rings.	Place *unwashed* peppers in a plastic bag and refrigerate. Store *green peppers* for up to 5 days and *red peppers* for up to 3 days.
POTATOES - Choose firm potatoes with reasonably smooth skins. Avoid those with sprouting eyes, soft black spots or green areas.	Wash and scrub well. Peel, if desired. Submerge peeled or sliced potatoes in cold water immediately after cutting to prevent discoloration. To bake, leave whole and unpeeled, and pierce in several places.	Store *unwashed*, in a cool (50°F.), dry, dark place with good ventilation for up to 2 months or at room temperature for up to 1 week.
SQUASH (summer - crookneck, patty-pan or zucchini) - Select firm, small to medium squash with smooth, glossy tender skin. Squash should feel heavy for their size.	Trim ends and rinse. *Do not peel.* Leave whole, dice or cut into strips or slices.	Store *unwashed* squash in a perforated plastic bag and refrigerate for up to 5 days.
TOMATOES - Choose tomatoes that are smooth, well-formed and firm but not hard. Color varies according to variety.	Wash. Cut out stem. Peel, if desired, by submerging tomato into boiling water 30 seconds then immediately into cold water. To seed, slice in half crosswise and squeeze out seeds. Leave whole, slice, chop or quarter.	Store *unwashed* tomatoes at room temperature, stem end down, until slightly soft. Refrigerate very ripe tomatoes, *unwrapped,* for up to 4 days.

For easy entertaining or to add flair to your next family get-together, look to CAMPBELL'S Soups to perk up ordinary foods in minutes. From light, savory *Tortilla Vegetable Bites* and *Salsa Onion Dip* to heartier *Souper Mushroom Pizza* and *Onion Chicken Nuggets,* these quick-and-easy finger foods are certain to provide a mouthwatering beginning to mealtime or anytime. Here you'll also find CAMPBELL'S most requested recipe, *Tomato Soup Cake.* Popular since the 1920s, it's delicious eaten at snack time and for dessert.

Clockwise from top: Fiesta Nachos (page 27), Shrimp Dip (page 23) and Tortilla Vegetable Bites (page 20).

Souper Mushroom Pizza

To release more flavor, be sure to crush measured dried herbs or seasonings with your fingers before adding to recipe.

1 loaf (about 1 pound) Italian bread (16-inches long),
    cut in half lengthwise
1 can (10¾ ounces) CAMPBELL'S condensed Cream of Mushroom Soup
¼ teaspoon garlic powder
¼ teaspoon Italian seasoning, crushed
1 cup shredded mozzarella cheese (4 ounces)
1 tablespoon grated Parmesan cheese
1 small red pepper, chopped (about ½ cup)
2 green onions, chopped (about ¼ cup)

- Bake bread on baking sheet at 400° F. for 5 minutes or until lightly toasted.
- Mix soup, garlic powder and Italian seasoning. Stir in mozzarella cheese, Parmesan cheese, pepper and onions.
- Spread soup mixture on bread. Bake 5 minutes or until cheese is melted. Cut each bread half into 12 slices.

Makes 24 appetizers
Prep Time: 15 minutes
Cook Time: 5 minutes

Tortilla Vegetable Bites

1 package (8 ounces) cream cheese, softened
1 pouch CAMPBELL'S Dry Onion Soup and Recipe Mix
1 teaspoon Louisiana-style hot sauce
1 small carrot, shredded (about ⅓ cup)
2 green onions, chopped (about ¼ cup)
6 flour tortillas (8-inch)

- Stir cream cheese until smooth. Stir in soup mix, hot sauce, carrot and onions. Top each tortilla with about ¼ *cup* cheese mixture. Spread to edge. Tightly roll up like a jelly roll. Place seam-side down in large shallow dish. Cover and refrigerate at least 2 hours.
- Cut each roll-up into 1-inch slices.

Makes 36 appetizers
Prep Time: 15 minutes
Chill Time: 2 hours

Souper Mushroom Pizza

*C*hili powder
is a blend of
ground dried
chilies, cumin,
coriander, cloves,
oregano and gar-
lic. Red spices like
chili powder and
paprika retain
their color and
flavor best when
stored tightly
sealed in the
refrigerator.

M EXICALI DIP

  1   **can (11½ ounces) CAMPBELL'S condensed Bean with Bacon Soup**
 ½ **cup sour cream**
  1   **teaspoon chili powder**
 ½ **cup PACE Thick & Chunky Salsa**
  1   **cup shredded Cheddar cheese (4 ounces)**
     Sliced green onions
     Sliced VLASIC *or* EARLY CALIFORNIA pitted Ripe Olives
     Tortilla chips

●   Mix soup, sour cream and chili powder. Spread in microwave-safe
      10-inch plate. Top with salsa, cheese, onions and olives. Microwave dip
      mixture on HIGH 2 minutes. Serve with tortilla chips for dipping.

Makes 1½ cups
Prep Time: 15 minutes
Cook Time: 2 minutes

Mexicali Dip (left), Cape
Cod Dip (right)

CAPE COD DIP

1 package (8 ounces) cream cheese, softened
1 can (10¾ ounces) CAMPBELL'S condensed New England Clam Chowder
½ teaspoon Worcestershire sauce
¼ teaspoon garlic powder
⅛ teaspoon Louisiana-style hot sauce
  Fresh vegetables, crackers *or* chips

- Stir cream cheese until smooth. Stir in soup, Worcestershire, garlic powder and hot sauce. Refrigerate at least 2 hours. Serve with crackers, chips or fresh vegetables for dipping. If desired, garnish with *fresh chives*.

Makes 2 cups
Prep Time: 5 minutes
Chill Time: 2 hours

SHRIMP DIP

1 package (8 ounces) cream cheese, softened
1 can (10¾ ounces) CAMPBELL'S condensed Cream of Shrimp Soup
½ teaspoon Louisiana-style hot sauce
¼ cup finely chopped celery
1 tablespoon finely chopped onion
  Fresh vegetables, crackers *or* chips

- Stir cream cheese until smooth. Stir in soup, hot sauce, celery and onion. Refrigerate at least 4 hours. Serve with fresh vegetables, crackers or chips for dipping. If desired, garnish with *green pepper*.

Makes 2¼ cups
Prep Time: 10 minutes
Chill Time: 4 hours

To soften 8 ounces cream cheese, remove from wrapper. On microwave-safe plate, microwave on HIGH 15 seconds.

$\mathcal{O}$NION CHICKEN NUGGETS

1 **pouch CAMPBELL'S Dry Onion Soup and Recipe Mix**
²/₃ **cup dry bread crumbs**
¹/₈ **teaspoon pepper**
1 **egg or 2 egg whites**
2 **tablespoons water**
1¹/₂ **pounds skinless, boneless chicken breasts or thighs,**
   cut into 1-inch pieces
2 **tablespoons margarine or butter,**
   melted (optional)
Dijon-style mustard

- Crush soup mix in pouch with rolling pin. Mix soup mix, bread crumbs and pepper on plate.
- Mix egg and water in shallow dish. Dip chicken into egg mixture. Coat with crumb mixture.
- Place chicken on baking sheet. Drizzle with margarine. Bake at 400° F. for 15 minutes or until chicken is no longer pink. Serve with mustard for dipping.

Serves 10 as an appetizer
Prep Time: 20 minutes
Cook Time: 15 minutes

$\mathcal{S}$ALSA ONION DIP

1 **pouch CAMPBELL'S Dry Onion Soup and Recipe Mix**
1 **container (16 ounces) sour cream**
1 **cup PACE Thick & Chunky Salsa**
Fresh vegetables and crackers

- Mix soup mix, sour cream and salsa. Refrigerate at least 2 hours. Serve with fresh vegetables and crackers for dipping. If desired, garnish with green onion.

Makes 3 cups
Prep Time: 5 minutes
Chill Time: 2 hours

$\mathcal{U}$se a sturdy plastic cutting board instead of a wooden board when cutting raw poultry. Since wood boards are porous, it's difficult to thoroughly wash them.

Onion Chicken Nuggets (top), Salsa Onion Dip (bottom)

OSTADAS

8 flour tortillas (8-inch)
1 can (11 1/8 ounces) **CAMPBELL'S condensed Fiesta Tomato Soup**
1 cup shredded **Cheddar cheese (4 ounces)**
1 cup shredded **mozzarella cheese (4 ounces)**
   Sliced green onion (optional)
   Sliced VLASIC or **EARLY CALIFORNIA pitted Ripe Olives (optional)**

- Place tortillas on 2 large baking sheets. Top each tortilla with about 2 *tablespoons* soup. Spread to within 1/2 inch of edge. Top with cheeses, onion and olives.
- Bake at 400°F. for 10 minutes or until tortillas are crisp. Cut each tostada into quarters.

Makes 32 appetizers
Prep Time: 10 minutes
Cook Time: 10 minutes

IESTA NACHOS

1 can (11 ounces) **CAMPBELL'S condensed Fiesta Nacho Cheese Soup**
1/3 cup **water**
1 bag (about 10 ounces) **tortilla chips**
   Chopped tomato
   Sliced green onions
   Sliced VLASIC or **EARLY CALIFORNIA pitted Ripe Olives**
   Chopped green and/or **red pepper**

- In small saucepan mix soup and water. Over low heat, heat through, stirring often.
- Serve over tortilla chips. Top with tomato, onions, olives and pepper.

Serves 6
Prep Time: 10 minutes
Cook Time: 5 minutes

*C*hoose clean bunches of green onions or scallions with firm, white roots and crisp, green tops. Avoid ones with browned roots and wilted tops.

Tostadas

TOMATO SOUP CAKE

2	cups all-purpose flour
1 1/3	cups sugar
4	teaspoons baking powder
1 1/2	teaspoons ground allspice
1	teaspoon baking soda
1	teaspoon ground cinnamon
1/2	teaspoon ground cloves
1	can (10 3/4 ounces) CAMPBELL'S condensed Tomato Soup
1/2	cup vegetable shortening
2	eggs
1/4	cup water

- Preheat oven to 350°F. Grease and lightly flour 13-by 9-inch baking pan. Set aside.
- In large bowl mix flour, sugar, baking powder, allspice, baking soda, cinnamon and cloves. Add soup, shortening, eggs and water. With mixer at low speed, beat until well mixed, constantly scraping side and bottom of bowl. At high speed, beat 4 minutes, occasionally scraping bowl. Pour into prepared pan.
- Bake 40 minutes or until toothpick inserted in center comes out clean. Cool in pan on wire rack 10 minutes. Remove from pan and cool completely on rack. Frost with Cream Cheese Frosting.

Serves 12
Prep Time: 20 minutes
Cook Time: 40 minutes
Cool Time: 30 minutes

CREAM CHEESE FROSTING

1	package (8 ounces) cream cheese, softened
2	tablespoons milk
1	teaspoon vanilla extract
1	package (16 ounces) confectioners' sugar (about 4 cups)

- In medium bowl with mixer at medium speed, beat cream cheese, milk and vanilla until creamy. Gradually beat in sugar until frosting is smooth.

Makes 3 cups
Prep Time: 10 minutes

This moist spice cake was first made with canned tomatoes, but the tomatoes were replaced with condensed tomato soup in the 1920s. Today, this delicious cake is CAMPBELL'S most requested recipe.

Tomato Soup Cake

Great for potlucks and family dinners, casseroles and bakes are easy to make and even easier to eat. Little preparation and quick clean-up makes these one-dish meals a favorite choice, especially during the busy workweek. *One-Dish Chicken & Rice Bake, Easy Party Lasagna* and a variety of other timesaving recipes included here provide delicious ways to enjoy a home cooked meal with ease. With CAMPBELL'S Soup as the secret ingredient, your family will enjoy great-tasting, home-style flavor every time you cook.

Crunchy Chicken Bake, top, (page 37) and Easy Party Lasagna, bottom, (page 37).

ONE-DISH CHICKEN & STUFFING BAKE

1¼ **cups boiling water**

4 **tablespoons margarine *or* butter, melted***

4 **cups PEPPERIDGE FARM Herb Seasoned Stuffing**

4 **to 6 skinless, boneless chicken breast halves (about 1 to 1½ pounds)**
   Paprika

1 **can (10¾ ounces) CAMPBELL'S condensed Cream of Mushroom Soup**

⅓ **cup milk**

1 **tablespoon chopped fresh parsley *or* 1 teaspoon dried parsley flakes**

- Mix water and margarine. Add stuffing. Mix lightly.
- Spoon stuffing across center of 3-quart shallow baking dish, leaving space on both sides for chicken. Arrange chicken on each side of stuffing. Sprinkle paprika over chicken.
- Mix soup, milk and parsley. Pour over chicken.
- Cover and bake at 400° F. for 30 minutes or until chicken is no longer pink. If desired, garnish with additional *fresh parsley*.

Serves 4 to 6

Prep Time: 10 minutes

Cook Time: 30 minutes

*For lower fat stuffing, reduce margarine to 1 tablespoon.

Tip: To melt margarine, remove wrapper and place in microwave-safe cup. Cover and microwave on HIGH 45 seconds.

*T*his easy casserole can also be made with cubed stuffing: Substitute 4 cups PEPPERIDGE FARM Cubed Herb Seasoned Stuffing for Herb Seasoned Stuffing.

One-Dish Chicken & Stuffing Bake

CHEDDAR-SWISS STRATA

    6 cups French *or* Italian bread cut in 1-inch cubes
    1 can (10 ¾ ounces) CAMPBELL'S condensed Cheddar Cheese Soup
    1 cup milk
    4 eggs, beaten
1 ½ cups shredded Swiss cheese (6 ounces)

- Arrange bread cubes in greased 2-quart shallow baking dish. Mix soup, milk and eggs. Add cheese. Pour over bread. Cover and refrigerate overnight.
- Uncover. Bake at 350°F. for 40 minutes or until knife inserted near center comes out clean. If desired, garnish with *fresh chives* and *thyme*.

Serves 8
Prep Time: 15 minutes
Chill Time: 24 hours
Cook Time: 40 minutes

CHICKEN-BROCCOLI DIVAN

    1 pound broccoli, cut into spears, cooked and drained
1 ½ cups cubed cooked chicken *or* turkey
    1 can (10 ¾ ounces) CAMPBELL'S condensed Cream of Broccoli Soup
  ⅓ cup milk
  ½ cup shredded Cheddar cheese (2 ounces)
    2 tablespoons dry bread crumbs
    1 tablespoon margarine *or* butter, melted

- In 9-inch pie plate or 2-quart shallow baking dish arrange broccoli and chicken. In small bowl mix soup and milk and pour over broccoli and chicken.
- Sprinkle cheese over soup mixture. Mix bread crumbs with margarine and sprinkle over cheese. Bake at 450° F. for 20 minutes or until hot.

Serves 4
Prep Time: 15 minutes
Cook Time: 20 minutes

A great brunch or buffet dish, Cheddar-Swiss Strata can be easily doubled to serve 16. Double all ingredients. Divide ingredients evenly between two 2-quart shallow baking dishes and bake as directed.

Cheddar-Swiss Strata

To destroy any bacteria that might be present in ground meat, it's important to cook it thoroughly. When preparing a meat loaf, use a meat thermometer to make sure it cooks to 160°F.

BEST-EVER MEAT LOAF

1 can (11 1/8 ounces) **CAMPBELL'S** condensed Italian Tomato Soup
2 pounds ground beef
1 pouch **CAMPBELL'S** Dry Onion Soup and Recipe Mix
1/2 cup dry bread crumbs
1 egg, beaten
1/4 cup water

- Mix 1/2 *cup* Italian tomato soup, beef, soup mix, bread crumbs and egg *thoroughly.* In medium baking pan shape *firmly* into 8-by 4-inch loaf.
- Bake at 350°F. for 1 1/4 hours or until meat loaf is no longer pink (160°F.).
- In small saucepan mix 2 *tablespoons* drippings, remaining soup and water. Heat through. Serve with meat loaf.

Serves 8
Prep Time: 10 minutes
Cook Time: 1 hour 20 minutes

Easy Party Lasagna

1 can (10 ¾ ounces) CAMPBELL'S condensed Cream of Mushroom Soup
¼ cup milk
2 cups shredded mozzarella cheese (8 ounces)
1 pound ground beef
1 can (11 ⅛ ounces) CAMPBELL'S condensed Italian Tomato Soup
1 cup water
6 *dry* lasagna noodles

- Mix mushroom soup, milk and ½ *cup* cheese. Set aside.
- In medium skillet over medium-high heat, cook beef until browned, stirring to separate meat. Pour off fat. Stir in Italian tomato soup and water. Heat through.
- In 2-quart shallow baking dish spoon *half* the meat mixture. Top with 3 lasagna noodles and mushroom soup mixture. Top with remaining 3 lasagna noodles and remaining meat mixture. Cover.
- Bake at 400° F. for 40 minutes or until hot. Uncover and sprinkle remaining cheese over top. Bake 10 minutes more or until cheese is melted. Let stand 10 minutes. If desired, garnish with *fresh basil*.

Serves 8
Prep Time: 20 minutes
Cook Time: 50 minutes
Stand Time: 10 minutes

Crunchy Chicken Bake

8 skinless, boneless chicken breast halves (about 2 pounds)
4 slices Swiss cheese (about 4 ounces), cut in half
1 can (10¾ ounces) CAMPBELL'S condensed Cream of Broccoli Soup
1 large tomato, cut into 8 slices
½ cup PEPPERIDGE FARM Herb Seasoned Stuffing, crushed
2 tablespoons margarine *or* butter, melted
8 cups hot cooked rice

- Place chicken in 3-quart shallow baking dish. Top with cheese. Spoon soup over cheese. Arrange tomato over soup. Mix stuffing and margarine and sprinkle over tomato.
- Bake at 400° F. for 25 minutes or until chicken is no longer pink. Serve with rice. If desired, garnish with *fresh parsley*.

Serves 8
Prep Time: 10 minutes
Cook Time: 25 minutes

*G*round meats are more perishable than other types and should be used within one to two days.

In addition to baking to a golden brown, check biscuits for doneness with a toothpick. When inserted in the center of a biscuit, the toothpick should come out clean.

VEGETABLE BEEF & BISCUIT CASSEROLE

1 1/2 pounds ground beef
1 can (10 3/4 ounces) **CAMPBELL'S** condensed Tomato Soup
1 can (10 3/4 ounces) **CAMPBELL'S** condensed Golden Corn Soup
3/4 cup water
1 tablespoon Worcestershire sauce
1 can (15 ounces) mixed vegetables, drained
1 package (7 1/2 or 10 ounces) refrigerated buttermilk biscuits (10 biscuits)
1/2 cup shredded Cheddar cheese (2 ounces)

- In medium skillet over medium-high heat, cook beef until browned, stirring to separate meat. Pour off fat.
- Add soups, water, Worcestershire and vegetables. Spoon into 3-quart shallow baking dish. Bake at 400° F. for 10 minutes or until hot.
- Stir. Arrange biscuits over beef mixture. Top with cheese. Bake 15 minutes more or until biscuits are golden.

Serves 6
Prep Time: 15 minutes
Cook Time: 25 minutes

EASY CHICKEN & BISCUITS

1 can (10 3/4 ounces) **CAMPBELL'S** condensed Cream of Celery Soup
1 can (10 3/4 ounces) **CAMPBELL'S** condensed Cream of Potato Soup
1 cup milk
1/4 teaspoon dried thyme leaves, crushed
1/4 teaspoon pepper
4 cups cooked cut-up vegetables*
2 cups cubed cooked chicken or ham
1 package (7 1/2 or 10 ounces) refrigerated buttermilk biscuits (10 biscuits)

- In 3-quart shallow baking dish mix soups, milk, thyme, pepper, vegetables and chicken.
- Bake at 400° F. for 15 minutes or until hot.
- Stir. Arrange biscuits over chicken mixture. Bake 15 minutes more or until biscuits are golden.

Serves 5
Prep Time: 15 minutes
Cook Time: 30 minutes

* Use a combination of broccoli flowerets, cauliflower flowerets and sliced carrots.

Vegetable Beef & Biscuit
Casserole

Ranchero Macaroni Bake

1 can (26 ounces) CAMPBELL'S condensed Cream of Mushroom Soup
1 cup milk
1 cup PACE Thick & Chunky Salsa
3 cups shredded Cheddar *or* Monterey Jack cheese (12 ounces)
6 cups hot cooked elbow macaroni (about 3 cups dry)
1 cup coarsely crushed tortilla chips

- Mix soup, milk, salsa, cheese and macaroni. Spoon into 3-quart shallow baking dish.
- Bake at 400° F. for 20 minutes or until hot.
- Stir. Sprinkle chips over macaroni mixture. Bake 5 minutes more.

Serves 8 as a main dish or 12 as a side dish
Prep Time: 20 minutes
Cook Time: 25 minutes

One-Dish Chicken & Rice Bake

1 can (10 3/4 ounces) CAMPBELL'S condensed Cream of Mushroom Soup
1 cup water
3/4 cup uncooked regular long-grain rice
1/4 teaspoon paprika
1/4 teaspoon pepper
4 skinless, boneless chicken breast halves (about 1 pound)

- In 2-quart shallow baking dish mix soup, water, rice, paprika and pepper. Place chicken on rice mixture. Sprinkle with additional paprika and pepper.
- Cover. Bake at 375°F. for 45 minutes or until chicken is no longer pink and rice is done.

Serves 4
Prep Time: 5 minutes
Cook Time: 45 minutes

When cooking pasta, use a large saucepot or Dutch oven and at least 4 quarts of water per pound of dry pasta. Bring water to a rapid boil and cook pasta, uncovered, stirring frequently to keep pieces separate.

Ranchero Macaroni Bake

CHICKEN ENCHILADAS

*S*hort on time?
Use two cans
(5 ounces *each*)
SWANSON
Premium Chunk
Chicken, drained,
for the 2 cups
chopped cooked
chicken.

1   can (10 ¾ ounces) **CAMPBELL'S** condensed Cream of Chicken Soup
½   cup sour cream
1   tablespoon margarine *or* butter
1   medium onion, chopped (about ½ cup)
1   teaspoon chili powder
2   cups chopped cooked chicken *or* turkey
1   can (about 4 ounces) chopped green chilies
8   flour tortillas (8-inch)
1   cup shredded **Cheddar** *or* **Monterey Jack** cheese (4 ounces)

- In small bowl mix soup and sour cream.
- In medium saucepan over medium heat, heat margarine. Add onion and chili powder. Cook until tender. Add chicken, chilies and 2 *tablespoons* soup mixture.
- Spread ½ *cup* soup mixture in 2-quart shallow baking dish. Along one side of each tortilla, spread about ¼ *cup* chicken mixture. Roll up each tortilla around filling and place seam-side down in baking dish.
- Spread remaining soup mixture over enchiladas. Sprinkle cheese over soup mixture. Bake at 350° F. for 25 minutes or until hot.

Serves 4
Prep Time: 25 minutes
Cook Time: 25 minutes

Chicken Enchiladas

*P*oultry dishes have always been popular with people on the go. A versatile, family-pleasing food, chicken can be prepared in a variety of ways to suit the occasion. From simple *Sweet & Sour Chicken* and *Chicken Rice Skillet* to dressier *Shortcut Chicken Cordon Bleu* and *Chicken Enchiladas,* poultry takes center stage at a sophisticated party or provides the perfect main-dish for today's busy families. CAMPBELL'S condensed Soups take away much of the work, guaranteeing rave reviews for even the newest of cooks. For sensational suppers in a snap, these flavorful poultry entrées will turn everyday fare into a memorable meal.

Chicken Dijon, top, (page 51) and Lemon Broccoli Chicken, bottom, (page 49).

CHICKEN IN SAVORY LEMON SAUCE

Vegetable cooking spray
4 skinless, boneless chicken breast halves (about 1 pound)
**1 can (10 ¾ ounces) CAMPBELL'S HEALTHY REQUEST condensed
    Cream of Chicken Soup**
2 tablespoons water
1 tablespoon chopped fresh parsley or 1 teaspoon dried parsley flakes
1 tablespoon lemon juice
½ teaspoon paprika
¼ cup chopped green or red pepper

- Spray medium skillet with cooking spray and heat over medium-high heat 1 minute. Add chicken and cook 10 minutes or until browned. Set chicken aside.
- Add soup, water, parsley, lemon juice, paprika and pepper. Heat to a boil. Return chicken to pan. Reduce heat to low. Cover and cook 5 minutes or until chicken is no longer pink. If desired, garnish with *lemon*.

Serves 4
Prep Time: 10 minutes
Cook Time: 20 minutes

To chop fresh parsley, rinse well and gently pat dry. Discard stems. Chop leaves with an 8-inch chef's knife or place the herb in a 1-cup glass measuring cup and snip it with kitchen scissors.

SKILLET HERB ROASTED CHICKEN

2 tablespoons all-purpose flour
¼ teaspoon ground sage
¼ teaspoon dried thyme leaves, crushed
4 skinless, boneless chicken breast halves (about 1 pound)
2 tablespoons margarine or butter
1 can (10 ¾ ounces) CAMPBELL'S condensed Cream of Celery Soup
½ cup water
4 cups hot cooked rice

- Mix flour, sage and thyme on plate. Coat chicken with flour mixture.
- In medium skillet over medium heat, heat margarine. Add chicken and cook 15 minutes or until chicken is browned and no longer pink. Remove and keep warm.
- Add soup and water. Reduce heat to low and heat through. Serve over chicken with rice.

Serves 4
Prep Time: 5 minutes
Cook Time: 20 minutes

Chicken in Savory
Lemon Sauce

*B*ecause raw poultry is highly perishable, store uncooked chicken in the coldest section of the refrigerator no longer than two days.

*E*ASY CHICKEN & PASTA

  1 **tablespoon vegetable oil**
  1 **pound skinless, boneless chicken breasts, cut up**
  1 **can (10¾ ounces) CAMPBELL'S condensed Cream of Chicken Soup**
½ **cup water**
  1 **bag (about 16 ounces) frozen seasoned pasta and vegetable combination**

- In medium skillet over medium-high heat, heat oil. Add chicken and cook until browned, stirring often. Set chicken aside.
- Add soup, water and vegetable combination. Heat to a boil. Return chicken to pan. Reduce heat to low. Cover and cook 5 minutes or until chicken is no longer pink, stirring occasionally. If desired, garnish with *fresh basil.*

Serves 4
Prep Time: 5 minutes
Cook Time: 20 minutes

*L*EMON BROCCOLI CHICKEN

 1 **lemon**
 1 **tablespoon vegetable oil**
 4 **skinless, boneless chicken breast halves (about 1 pound)**
 1 **can (10¾ ounces) CAMPBELL'S condensed Cream of Broccoli Soup**
¼ **cup milk**
⅛ **teaspoon pepper**

- Cut 4 thin slices of lemon and set aside. Squeeze 2 teaspoons juice from remaining lemon and set aside.
- In medium skillet over medium-high heat, heat oil. Add chicken and cook 10 minutes or until browned. Set chicken aside. Pour off fat.
- Add soup, milk, reserved lemon juice and pepper. Heat to a boil. Return chicken to pan. Top with lemon slices. Reduce heat to low. Cover and cook 5 minutes or until chicken is no longer pink. If desired, garnish with *fresh marjoram*.

Serves 4
Prep Time: 5 minutes
Cook Time: 20 minutes

*C*HICKEN CRUNCH

 1 **can (10¾ ounces) CAMPBELL'S condensed Cream of Chicken Soup**
½ **cup milk**
 4 **skinless, boneless chicken breast halves (about 1 pound)**
 2 **tablespoons all-purpose flour**
1½ **cups PEPPERIDGE FARM Herb Seasoned Stuffing, finely crushed**
 2 **tablespoons margarine *or* butter, melted**

- Mix ⅓ *cup* soup and ¼ *cup* milk in shallow dish. Lightly coat chicken with flour. Dip into soup mixture. Coat with stuffing.
- Place chicken on baking sheet. Drizzle with margarine. Bake at 400° F. for 20 minutes or until chicken is no longer pink.
- In small saucepan mix remaining soup and remaining milk. Over medium heat, heat through. Serve with chicken.

Serves 4
Prep Time: 15 minutes
Cook Time: 20 minutes

*W*hen shopping for skinless, boneless chicken breasts, the chicken should be light in color, not gray or pasty looking.

QUICK CHICKEN À LA KING

  1 **tablespoon margarine** *or* **butter**
 1/4 **cup chopped red** *or* **green pepper**
  1 **can (10¾ ounces) CAMPBELL'S condensed Cream of Mushroom Soup**
 1/2 **cup milk**
1½ **cups cubed cooked chicken** *or* **ham**
  4 **cups hot cooked long-grain and wild rice** *or* **hot cooked rice**

- In medium saucepan over medium heat, heat margarine. Add pepper and cook until tender.
- Add soup, milk and chicken. Heat through, stirring occasionally. Serve over rice. If desired, garnish with *fresh parsley*.

Serves 4
Prep Time: 10 minutes
Cook Time: 10 minutes

Souper-Quick Chicken à la King: Substitute 2 cans (5 ounces *each*) SWANSON Premium Chunk White *or* Chunk Chicken for cubed cooked chicken.

CHICKEN DIJON

 2 **tablespoons margarine** *or* **butter**
 4 **skinless, boneless chicken breast halves (about 1 pound)**
 1 **medium onion, chopped (about 1/2 cup)**
 1 **can (10¾ ounces) CAMPBELL'S condensed Cream of Chicken Soup**
1/4 **cup apple juice** *or* **milk**
 1 **tablespoon Dijon-style mustard**
 1 **tablespoon chopped fresh parsley** *or* **1 teaspoon dried parsley flakes**

- In medium skillet over medium-high heat, heat *half* the margarine. Add chicken and cook 10 minutes or until browned. Set chicken aside.
- Reduce heat to medium. Add remaining margarine. Add onion and cook until tender.
- Add soup, apple juice, mustard and parsley. Heat to a boil. Return chicken to pan. Reduce heat to low. Cover and cook 5 minutes or until chicken is no longer pink. If desired, garnish with additional *fresh parsley* and serve with *parslied noodles*.

Serves 4
Prep Time: 10 minutes
Cook Time: 25 minutes

*P*urchase red or green peppers, that are glossy, firm and well-shaped. Avoid peppers with soft spots and blemishes.

Quick Chicken à la King

CRISPY CHICKEN WITH ASPARAGUS SAUCE

4 skinless, boneless chicken breast halves *or* 8 skinless, boneless
  chicken thighs (about 1 pound)
1 egg *or* 2 egg whites, beaten
1/2 cup dry bread crumbs
2 tablespoons vegetable oil
1 can (10 3/4 ounces) **CAMPBELL'S** condensed Cream of Asparagus Soup
1/3 cup milk
1/3 cup water
  Parmesan cheese

- Dip chicken into egg. Coat with bread crumbs.
- In medium skillet over medium heat, heat oil. Add chicken and cook
  15 minutes or until chicken is browned and no longer pink. Remove and
  keep warm. Pour off fat.
- Add soup, milk and water. Reduce heat to low and heat through.
  Serve over chicken. Sprinkle with cheese. If desired, garnish with *fresh
  chives* and *lemon peel.*

Serves 4
Prep Time: 10 minutes
Cook Time: 20 minutes

ORIENTAL CHICKEN & VEGETABLE "STIR-FRY"

2 tablespoons cornstarch
1 can (14 1/2 ounces) **SWANSON** Oriental Broth
1 pound skinless, boneless chicken breasts, cut into strips
5 cups cut-up vegetables
4 cups hot cooked rice

- In bowl mix cornstarch and *1 cup* broth until smooth. Set aside.
- In medium nonstick skillet over medium-high heat, add chicken in
  2 batches and stir-fry until browned. Set chicken aside.
- Add remaining broth and vegetables. Heat to a boil. Reduce heat to
  low. Cover and cook 5 minutes or until vegetables are tender-crisp.
- Stir cornstarch mixture and add. Cook until mixture boils and
  thickens, stirring constantly. Return chicken to pan and heat through.
  Serve over rice.

Serves 4
Prep Time: 15 minutes
Cook Time: 25 minutes

To coat chicken, dip each piece into egg mixture, allowing excess to drip back into dish. In plastic bag or shallow dish, place bread crumbs. Coat both sides of chicken evenly, shaking off excess crumbs.

Crispy Chicken with
Asparagus Sauce

CHICKEN RICE SKILLET

1 tablespoon vegetable oil
2 pounds chicken parts
1 can (10 1/2 ounces) CAMPBELL'S condensed Chicken Broth
1/4 teaspoon garlic powder *or* 2 cloves garlic, minced
1/4 teaspoon hot pepper sauce (optional)
1 large green pepper, chopped (about 1 cup)
3/4 cup drained cut-up canned tomatoes *or* 1 small tomato, chopped (about 1/2 cup)
2/3 cup uncooked regular long-grain rice

- In medium skillet over medium-high heat, heat oil. Add chicken and cook 10 minutes or until browned. Set chicken aside. Pour off fat.
- Add broth, garlic powder, hot pepper sauce, green pepper, tomatoes and rice. Heat to a boil. Return chicken to pan. Reduce heat to low. Cover and cook 30 minutes or until chicken is no longer pink and rice is done.

Serves 4
Prep Time: 10 minutes
Cook Time: 45 minutes

Tip: If desired, remove skin from chicken before browning.

EASY CHICKEN PAPRIKASH

1 tablespoon margarine *or* butter
4 skinless, boneless chicken breast halves (about 1 pound)
1 can (10 3/4 ounces) CAMPBELL'S condensed Cream of Mushroom Soup
2 teaspoons paprika
1/8 teaspoon ground red pepper
1/3 cup sour cream *or* plain yogurt
4 cups hot cooked medium egg noodles (about 4 cups dry)

- In medium skillet over medium-high heat, heat margarine. Add chicken and cook 10 minutes or until browned. Set chicken aside.
- Add soup, paprika and pepper. Heat to a boil. Return chicken to pan. Reduce heat to low. Cover and cook 5 minutes or until chicken is no longer pink.
- Stir in sour cream and heat through. Serve with noodles.

Serves 4
Prep Time: 5 minutes
Cook Time: 25 minutes

*R*ice may be stored on the pantry shelf for two years when kept in an airtight container.

*S*HORTCUT CHICKEN CORDON BLEU

- 1 **tablespoon margarine** *or* **butter**
- 4 **skinless, boneless chicken breast halves (about 1 pound)**
- 1 **can (10 ¾ ounces) CAMPBELL'S condensed Cream of Chicken Soup**
- 2 **tablespoons water**
- 2 **tablespoons Chablis** *or* **other dry white wine**
- ½ **cup shredded Swiss cheese (2 ounces)**
- ½ **cup chopped cooked ham**
- 4 **cups hot cooked medium egg noodles (about 4 cups dry)**

- In medium skillet over medium-high heat, heat margarine. Add chicken and cook 10 minutes or until browned. Set chicken aside.
- Add soup, water, wine, cheese and ham. Heat to a boil, stirring often. Return chicken to pan. Reduce heat to low. Cover and cook 5 minutes or until chicken is no longer pink, stirring occasionally. Serve with noodles. If desired, garnish with *fresh thyme* and *green onion*.

Serves 4
Prep Time: 10 minutes
Cook Time: 20 minutes

ALL-AMERICAN BARBECUED CHICKEN

1 can (10 3/4 ounces) **CAMPBELL'S** condensed Tomato Soup
2 tablespoons honey
1 teaspoon dry mustard
1/2 teaspoon onion powder
4 chicken breast halves (about 2 pounds), skinned

- Mix soup, honey, mustard and onion powder.
- Place chicken on lightly oiled grill rack over medium-hot coals. Grill uncovered 20 minutes, turning often. Brush with soup mixture and grill 20 minutes more or until chicken is no longer pink, turning and brushing often with soup mixture.

Serves 4
Prep Time: 10 minutes
Cook Time: 40 minutes

Broiled All-American Barbecued Chicken: Prepare as in first step. Place chicken on rack in broiler pan. Broil 6 inches from heat 30 minutes or until chicken is no longer pink, turning and brushing often with soup mixture.

The temperature of the coals can be determined by holding the palm of your hand above the coals at the height the food is to be cooked. For medium-hot, you should be able to hold your hand in that position for 3 seconds before the heat forces you to pull it away.

$\mathcal{S}$WEET & SOUR CHICKEN

$\mathcal{S}$tir-fry means to cook sliced foods in a little oil or liquid while constantly stirring or tossing the food.

  3 **tablespoons cornstarch**
  I **can (10 $\frac{1}{2}$ ounces) CAMPBELL'S condensed Chicken Broth**
  I **tablespoon vegetable oil**
  I **pound skinless, boneless chicken breasts, cut into 1-inch pieces**
  I **can (8 ounces) pineapple chunks in juice, undrained**
$\frac{1}{4}$ **cup sugar**
$\frac{1}{4}$ **cup vinegar**
  I **small green *and/or* red pepper, cut into 2-inch-long strips (about I cup)**
  4 **cups hot cooked rice**

- In bowl mix cornstarch and broth until smooth. Set aside.
- In medium skillet over medium-high heat, heat oil. Add chicken in 2 batches and stir-fry until browned. Set chicken aside. Pour off fat.
- Reduce heat to medium. Add pineapple, sugar, vinegar and pepper. Heat to a boil. Stir cornstarch mixture and add. Cook until mixture boils and thickens, stirring constantly.
- Return chicken to pan. Reduce heat to low. Cover and cook 5 minutes or until chicken is no longer pink, stirring occasionally. Serve over rice.

Serves 4
Prep Time: 15 minutes
Cook Time: 25 minutes

$\mathcal{S}$AUTÉED CHICKEN BREASTS

  2 **tablespoons all-purpose flour**
$\frac{1}{8}$ **teaspoon pepper**
  4 **skinless, boneless chicken breast halves (about I pound)**
  2 **tablespoons vegetable oil**
  I **can (11 $\frac{1}{8}$ ounces) CAMPBELL'S condensed Italian Tomato Soup**
$\frac{1}{2}$ **cup water**

- Mix flour and pepper on plate. Coat chicken with flour mixture.
- In medium skillet over medium-high heat, heat oil. Add chicken and cook 10 minutes or until browned. Set chicken aside. Pour off fat.
- Add soup and water. Heat to a boil. Return chicken to pan. Reduce heat to low. Cover and cook 5 minutes or until chicken is no longer pink.

Serves 4
Prep Time: 10 minutes
Cook Time: 20 minutes

Sweet & Sour Chicken

*H*ERB BROILED CHICKEN

    1 can (10 ½ ounces) CAMPBELL'S condensed Chicken Broth
    3 tablespoons lemon juice
    1 teaspoon dried basil leaves, crushed
    1 teaspoon dried thyme leaves, crushed
  ⅛ teaspoon pepper
    2 pounds chicken parts

- Mix broth, lemon juice, basil, thyme and pepper.
- Place chicken on rack in broiler pan. Broil 6 inches from heat 30 minutes or until chicken is no longer pink, turning and brushing often with broth mixture. If desired, garnish with *fresh basil.*

Serves 4
Prep Time: 10 minutes
Cook Time: 30 minutes

Tip: If desired, remove skin from chicken before broiling.

*T*o broil 6 inches from heat, use a ruler to measure the distance between the food's surface and the broiler element.

*S*AVORY SKILLET CHICKEN & RICE

    1 tablespoon margarine *or* butter
    1 pound skinless, boneless chicken breasts, cut up
    1 can (10 ¾ ounces) CAMPBELL'S condensed Cream of Mushroom Soup
    1 cup milk
    1 tablespoon onion flakes
  ¼ teaspoon dried thyme leaves, crushed
  ⅛ teaspoon pepper
    1 can (about 16 ounces) cut green beans, drained
    2 cups uncooked instant rice

- In medium skillet over medium-high heat, heat margarine. Add chicken and cook until browned, stirring often. Set chicken aside.
- Add soup, milk, onion flakes, thyme and pepper. Heat to a boil. Return chicken to pan. Reduce heat to low. Cover and cook 5 minutes or until chicken is no longer pink.
- Stir in beans and rice. Cover and remove from heat. Let stand 5 minutes. Fluff with fork.

Serves 4
Prep Time: 5 minutes
Cook Time: 20 minutes
Stand Time: 5 minutes

Herb Broiled Chicken

*S*tir-fried, baked or grilled, this bevy of beef dishes is certain to make your next meal a sizzling success. From hearty *Beef Stroganoff* to zesty *Italian Pepper Steak*, these main-dish recipes can be prepared in practically no time, promising you hassle free cooking. Family favorites, like kid-pleasing *Beefy Macaroni Skillet* and hearty *Simple Salisbury Steak,* provide a way to cater to everyone in the household. These delicious, full-flavored specialties are sure to satisfy even the heartiest appetites. Relax. No one will have a beef with these great-tasting recipes!

Beef & Mushrooms Dijon, top, (page 73) and Foolproof Beef & Broccoli, bottom, (page 64).

Beefy Mac 'n' Corn

To chop an onion, trim ends and peel outer skin. Halve onion from top to root end. Place halves flat side down; make parallel vertical slices. Then cut across the slices.

- 1 **pound ground beef**
- 1 **medium onion, chopped (about $1/2$ cup)**
- 1 **can (10 $3/4$ ounces) CAMPBELL'S condensed Golden Corn Soup**
- 1 **can (11 $1/8$ ounces) CAMPBELL'S condensed Italian Tomato Soup**
- $1/4$ **cup water**
- 1 **teaspoon Worcestershire sauce**
- $1/8$ **teaspoon pepper**
- 2 **cups cooked elbow macaroni (about 1 cup dry)**
  Parmesan cheese

- In medium skillet over medium-high heat, cook beef and onion until beef is browned, stirring to separate meat. Pour off fat.
- Add soups, water, Worcestershire, pepper and macaroni. Reduce heat to low and heat through. Serve with cheese.

Serves 5
Prep Time: 15 minutes
Cook Time: 10 minutes

Foolproof Beef & Broccoli

- 1 **pound boneless beef sirloin *or* top round steak, $3/4$ inch thick**
- 2 **tablespoons vegetable oil**
- 2 **cups broccoli flowerets**
- 1 **medium onion, cut into wedges**
- $1/8$ **teaspoon garlic powder *or* 1 clove garlic, minced**
- 1 **can (10 $3/4$ ounces) CAMPBELL'S condensed Cream of Broccoli Soup**
- $1/3$ **cup water**
- 1 **tablespoon soy sauce**
- 4 **cups hot cooked rice**

- Slice beef into very thin strips.
- In medium skillet over medium-high heat, heat *half* the oil. Add beef in 2 batches and stir-fry until browned. Set beef aside.
- Reduce heat to medium. Add remaining oil. Add broccoli, onion and garlic powder and stir-fry until tender-crisp.
- Add soup, water and soy. Heat to a boil. Return beef to pan and heat through. Serve over rice. If desired, garnish with *green onion*.

Serves 4
Prep Time: 15 minutes
Cook Time: 25 minutes

Beefy Mac 'n' Corn

$\mathcal{B}$EEF STROGANOFF

- 1 pound boneless beef sirloin *or* top round steak, ³/₄ inch thick
- 2 tablespoons vegetable oil
- 1 medium onion, chopped (about ¹/₂ cup)
- 1 can (10 ³/₄ ounces) **CAMPBELL'S** condensed Cream of Mushroom Soup
- ¹/₂ teaspoon paprika
- ¹/₂ cup sour cream *or* plain yogurt
- 4 cups hot cooked medium egg noodles (about 4 cups dry)

- Slice beef into very thin strips.
- In medium skillet over medium-high heat, heat *half* the oil. Add beef in 2 batches and cook until browned, stirring often. Set beef aside.
- Reduce heat to medium. Add remaining oil. Add onion and cook until tender. Pour off fat.
- Add soup and paprika. Heat to a boil. Stir in sour cream and return beef to pan. Heat through. Serve over noodles. If desired, garnish with *fresh parsley*.

Serves 4
Prep Time: 10 minutes
Cook Time: 25 minutes

$\mathcal{M}$ake slicing raw meat into thin strips easier by placing meat in freezer 1 hour or until meat is firm but not frozen.

$\mathcal{S}$KILLET MAC 'N' BEEF

- 1 pound ground beef
- 1 medium onion, chopped (about ¹/₂ cup)
- 1 can (10 ³/₄ ounces) **CAMPBELL'S** condensed Cream of Celery Soup
- ¹/₄ cup ketchup
- 1 tablespoon **Worcestershire** sauce
- 2 cups cooked corkscrew macaroni (about 1 ¹/₂ cups dry)

- In medium skillet over medium-high heat, cook beef and onion until beef is browned, stirring to separate meat. Pour off fat.
- Add soup, ketchup, Worcestershire and macaroni. Reduce heat to low and heat through.

Serves 4
Prep Time: 10 minutes
Cook Time: 15 minutes

Tip: Substitute 2 cups cooked elbow macaroni (about 1 cup dry) for corkscrew macaroni.

Beef Stroganoff

ITALIAN PEPPER STEAK

- 1 pound boneless beef sirloin *or* top round steak, ³/₄ inch thick
- 2 tablespoons olive *or* vegetable oil
- 2 small green *and/or* red peppers, cut into 2-inch-long strips (about 2 cups)
- 1 medium onion, sliced (about ¹/₂ cup)
- 1 teaspoon dried oregano leaves, crushed
- ¹/₄ teaspoon garlic powder *or* 2 cloves garlic, minced
- ¹/₄ teaspoon black pepper
- 1 can (11 ¹/₈ ounces) **CAMPBELL'S** condensed Italian Tomato Soup
- ¹/₂ cup water
- 4 cups hot cooked spaghetti (about 8 ounces dry)

- Slice beef into very thin strips.
- In medium skillet over medium-high heat, heat *half* the oil. Add beef in 2 batches and cook until browned, stirring often. Set beef aside.
- Reduce heat to medium. Add remaining oil. Add peppers, onion, oregano, garlic powder and black pepper and cook until tender.
- Add soup and water. Heat to a boil. Return beef to pan and heat through. Serve over spaghetti.

Serves 4
Prep Time: 15 minutes
Cook Time: 25 minutes

Tip: To make slicing easier, freeze beef 1 hour.

Sirloin really is "a cut above" because it comes from the upper part of the beef loin. Choose leaner cuts of beef like sirloin, top round or tenderloin and trim all visible fat before slicing or cooking.

Italian Pepper Steak

SPICY SALSA MAC & BEEF

1 **pound ground beef**
1 **can (10 $^1/_2$ ounces) CAMPBELL'S condensed Beef Broth**
1 **soup can water**
2 **cups dry medium shell macaroni or 2 cups dry elbow macaroni**
1 **can (10 $^3/_4$ ounces) CAMPBELL'S condensed Cheddar Cheese Soup**
1 **cup PACE Thick & Chunky Salsa**

- In medium skillet over medium-high heat, cook beef until browned, stirring to separate meat. Pour off fat.
- Add broth and water. Heat to a boil. Stir in macaroni. Reduce heat to medium. Cover and cook 10 minutes or until done, stirring often. Stir in soup and salsa. Heat through. If desired, garnish with *fresh parsley* and *shredded Cheddar cheese.*

Serves 4
Prep Time: 5 minutes
Cook Time: 25 minutes

BROCCOLI BEEF STIR-FRY

1 **pound boneless beef sirloin or top round steak, $^3/_4$ inch thick**
2 **tablespoons cornstarch**
1 **can (14 $^1/_2$ ounces) SWANSON Beef Broth**
2 **tablespoons soy sauce**
1 **tablespoon packed brown sugar**
2 **tablespoons vegetable oil**
4 **cups broccoli flowerets**
$^1/_4$ **teaspoon garlic powder or 2 cloves garlic, minced**
$^1/_4$ **teaspoon ground ginger**
4 **cups hot cooked rice**

- Slice beef into very thin strips. In bowl mix cornstarch, broth, soy and sugar until smooth. Set aside.
- In medium skillet over medium-high heat, heat *half* the oil. Add beef in 2 batches and stir-fry until browned. Set beef aside.
- Reduce heat to medium. Add remaining oil. Add broccoli, garlic powder and ginger and stir-fry until tender-crisp.
- Stir cornstarch mixture and add. Cook until mixture boils and thickens, stirring constantly. Return beef to pan and heat through. Serve over rice.

Serves 4
Prep Time: 15 minutes
Cook Time: 25 minutes

$\mathcal{M}$acaroni
may be stored on
the pantry shelf
for one year when
stored in an
airtight container.

Spicy Salsa Mac & Beef

When cooking pasta, be careful not to overcook it. Start testing for doneness at the *minimum* cooking time given on the package.

BEEFY MACARONI SKILLET

1	**pound ground beef**
1	**medium onion, chopped (about $^1/_2$ cup)**
1	**can (10$^3/_4$ ounces) CAMPBELL'S condensed Tomato Soup**
$^1/_4$	**cup water**
1	**tablespoon Worcestershire sauce**
$^1/_2$	**cup shredded Cheddar cheese (2 ounces)**
2	**cups cooked elbow twist *or* corkscrew macaroni (about 1$^1/_2$ cups dry)**

- In medium skillet over medium-high heat, cook beef and onion until beef is browned, stirring to separate meat. Pour off fat.
- Add soup, water, Worcestershire, cheese and macaroni. Reduce heat to low and heat through. If desired, garnish with *fresh parsley*.

Serves 4
Prep Time: 10 minutes
Cook Time: 15 minutes

BEEF & MUSHROOMS DIJON

- 1 **pound boneless beef sirloin *or* top round steak, $^3/_4$ inch thick**
- 2 **tablespoons vegetable oil**
- 2 **cups sliced mushrooms (about 6 ounces)**
- 1 **medium onion, sliced (about $^1/_2$ cup)**
- 1 **can (10$^3/_4$ ounces) CAMPBELL'S condensed Cream of Mushroom Soup**
- $^1/_2$ **cup water**
- 2 **tablespoons Dijon-style mustard**
- 4 **cups hot cooked rice**

- Slice beef into very thin strips.
- In medium skillet over medium-high heat, heat *half* the oil. Add beef in 2 batches and cook until browned, stirring often. Set beef aside.
- Reduce heat to medium. Add remaining oil. Add mushrooms and onion and cook until tender.
- Add soup, water and mustard. Heat to a boil. Return beef to pan and heat through. Serve over rice. If desired, garnish *fresh parsley*.

Serves 4
Prep Time: 15 minutes
Cook Time: 25 minutes

SIMPLE SALISBURY STEAK

- 1 **can (10$^3/_4$ ounces) CAMPBELL'S condensed Cream of Mushroom Soup**
- 1 **pound ground beef**
- $^1/_3$ **cup dry bread crumbs**
- 1 **small onion, finely chopped (about $^1/_4$ cup)**
- 1 **egg, beaten**
- 1 **tablespoon vegetable oil**
- 1$^1/_2$ **cups sliced mushrooms (about 4 ounces)**

- Mix $^1/_4$ *cup* soup, beef, bread crumbs, onion and egg *thoroughly*. Shape firmly into 4 patties, $^1/_2$ inch thick.
- In medium skillet over medium-high heat, heat oil. Cook patties until browned. Set patties aside. Pour off fat.
- Add remaining soup and mushrooms. Heat to a boil. Return patties to pan. Reduce heat to low. Cover and cook 20 minutes or until patties are no longer pink (160°F.).

Serves 4
Prep Time: 15 minutes
Cook Time: 35 minutes

*S*elect mushrooms that have caps that are firm, bright and bruise-free. The gills underneath should be tightly closed.

*I*TALIAN GRILLED BEEF

   1 **can (11 ⅛ ounces) CAMPBELL'S condensed Italian Tomato Soup**
  ½ **cup prepared Italian salad dressing**
1½ **pounds boneless beef sirloin steak, ¾ inch thick**

- Mix soup and dressing.
- Place steak on lightly oiled grill rack over medium-hot coals. Grill uncovered to desired doneness (allow 15 minutes for medium), turning once and brushing often with soup mixture.
- Heat remaining soup mixture to a boil and serve with steak.

Serves 6
Prep Time: 5 minutes
Cook Time: 15 minutes

Italian Grilled Beef Sandwiches: Prepare as in first and second steps. Slice steak into thin strips. In third step heat remaining soup mixture to a boil. Divide steak among 6 round sandwich rolls. Top with soup mixture. Makes 6 sandwiches.

*B*EEF & MOZZARELLA BAKE

   1 **pound ground beef**
   1 **can (11 ⅛ ounces) CAMPBELL'S condensed Italian Tomato Soup**
   1 **can (10 ¾ ounces) CAMPBELL'S condensed Cream of Mushroom Soup**
1¼ **cups water**
   1 **teaspoon dried basil leaves, crushed**
  ¼ **teaspoon pepper**
  ⅛ **teaspoon garlic powder *or* 1 clove garlic, minced**
1½ **cups shredded mozzarella cheese (6 ounces)**
   4 **cups hot cooked medium shell macaroni (about 3 cups dry)**

- In medium skillet over medium-high heat, cook beef until browned, stirring to separate meat. Pour off fat.
- Add soups, water, basil, pepper, garlic powder, *1 cup* cheese and macaroni. Spoon into 2-quart shallow baking dish. Bake at 400° F. for 20 minutes or until hot.
- Stir. Sprinkle remaining cheese over beef mixture. Bake 5 minutes more or until cheese is melted.

Serves 6
Prep Time: 15 minutes
Cook Time: 25 minutes

Italian Grilled Beef

*L*ooking for some great-tasting new ways to add pizzazz when preparing pork? With deliciously easy recipes, like *Honey-Barbecued Ribs, Harvest Pork Roast* and *Ham & Pasta Skillet*, you can feast on your favorite pork recipe without spending the day in the kitchen. CAMPBELL'S Soups help save you valuable time while delivering delicious home cooked flavor your family deserves. With this collection of extra-easy recipes, you can even prepare a sensational pork chop dinner any day of the week.

Pork Chop Skillet Dinner, top, (page 78) and Herbed Chops in Mushroom Sauce, bottom, (page 81).

BAKED PORK CHOPS WITH GARDEN STUFFING

A chop is a tender cut of pork, lamb or veal that has been taken from the loin or rib area. It may or may not be boneless.

- 1 can (10 ¾ ounces) CAMPBELL'S condensed Golden Mushroom Soup
- ¾ cup water
- 1 bag (16 ounces) frozen vegetable combination
- 1 tablespoon margarine *or* butter
- 4 cups PEPPERIDGE FARM Cubed Herb Seasoned Stuffing
- 6 pork chops, ¾ inch thick (about 2 pounds)

- In large saucepan mix ⅓ *cup soup*, ½ *cup water*, vegetables and margarine. Over medium heat, heat to a boil, stirring occasionally. Remove from heat. Add stuffing. Mix lightly.
- Spoon into greased 3-quart shallow baking dish. Arrange chops over stuffing.
- Mix remaining soup and water. Spoon over chops.
- Bake at 400° F. for 40 minutes or until chops are no longer pink. If desired, garnish with *fresh thyme* and *bay leaves*.

Serves 6
Prep Time: 10 minutes
Cook Time: 40 minutes

PORK CHOP SKILLET DINNER

- 1 tablespoon olive *or* vegetable oil
- 4 pork shoulder chops, ¾ inch thick (about 1 ½ pounds)
- 1 medium onion, chopped (about ½ cup)
- 1 cup uncooked regular long-grain rice
- 1 can (10 ½ ounces) CAMPBELL'S condensed Chicken Broth
- 1 cup orange juice
- 3 tablespoons chopped fresh parsley
- 4 orange slices

- In medium skillet over medium-high heat, heat oil. Add chops and cook 10 minutes or until browned. Set chops aside.
- Reduce heat to medium. Add onion. Add rice and cook until rice is browned, stirring constantly. Stir in broth, orange juice and 2 *tablespoons* parsley. Heat to a boil. Return chops to pan. Reduce heat to low. Cover and cook 20 minutes or until chops are no longer pink and rice is done.
- Top each chop with orange slice and sprinkle with remaining parsley. If desired, garnish with additional *fresh parsley*.

Serves 4
Prep Time: 10 minutes
Cook Time: 40 minutes

Baked Pork Chops with Garden Stuffing

*C*ooking pork
ribs in boiling
water before grilling
helps tenderize
the meat and
remove some of
the fat.

*H*ONEY-BARBECUED RIBS

 4 **pounds pork spareribs**
 I **pouch CAMPBELL'S Dry Onion Soup and Recipe Mix**
 $^3/_4$ **cup ketchup**
 $^3/_4$ **cup water**
 $^1/_3$ **cup honey**
 $^1/_2$ **teaspoon pepper**
 $^1/_4$ **teaspoon garlic powder *or* 2 cloves garlic, minced**

- In Dutch oven place ribs. Cover with water. Over high heat, heat to a boil. Reduce heat to low. Cover and cook 45 minutes. Drain.
- Meanwhile, in small saucepan mix soup mix, ketchup, water, honey, pepper and garlic powder. Over medium heat, heat to a boil. Reduce heat to low and cook 5 minutes, stirring occasionally.
- Place ribs on lightly oiled grill rack over medium-hot coals. Grill uncovered 30 minutes or until glazed, turning and brushing often with sauce. If desired, garnish with *fresh parsley*.

Serves 4
Prep Time: 10 minutes
Cook Time: I hour 15 minutes

Honey Oven-Barbecued Ribs: Prepare as in first and second steps. Arrange ribs in large shallow roasting pan. Pour sauce over ribs and turn to coat. Bake at 400 °F. for 20 minutes. Turn ribs and spoon sauce over ribs. Bake 20 minutes more or until glazed.

Herbed Chops in Mushroom Sauce

$\frac{1}{2}$ teaspoon garlic powder
$\frac{1}{2}$ teaspoon paprika
$\frac{1}{4}$ teaspoon dried basil leaves *or* dried thyme leaves, crushed
 4 boneless pork chops, $\frac{3}{4}$ inch thick (about 1 pound)
 1 tablespoon olive *or* vegetable oil
 1 medium onion, sliced (about $\frac{1}{2}$ cup)
 1 can (10 $\frac{3}{4}$ ounces) CAMPBELL'S condensed Cream of Mushroom Soup
$\frac{1}{4}$ cup milk
 4 cups hot cooked rice

- Mix garlic powder, paprika and basil on plate. Coat chops with seasoning mixture.
- In medium skillet over medium heat, heat oil. Add chops and cook 10 minutes or until browned. Set chops aside.
- Add onion and cook until tender.
- Add soup and milk. Heat to a boil. Return chops to pan. Reduce heat to low. Cover and cook 5 minutes or until chops are no longer pink. Serve with rice. If desired, garnish with *fresh basil*.

Serves 4
Prep Time: 10 minutes
Cook Time: 25 minutes

Saucy Tomato Pork Chops

 2 tablespoons all-purpose flour
$\frac{1}{4}$ teaspoon dried thyme leaves, crushed
 6 pork chops, $\frac{3}{4}$ inch thick (about 2 pounds)
 1 tablespoon vegetable oil
 1 can (10 $\frac{3}{4}$ ounces) CAMPBELL'S condensed Tomato Soup
$\frac{1}{4}$ cup water
 1 medium onion, sliced (about $\frac{1}{2}$ cup)

- Mix flour and thyme on plate. Coat chops with flour mixture.
- In medium skillet over medium-high heat, heat oil. Add chops in 2 batches and cook 10 minutes or until browned. Set chops aside. Pour off fat.
- Add soup, water and onion. Heat to a boil. Return chops to pan. Reduce heat to low. Cover and cook 10 minutes or until chops are no longer pink.

Serves 6
Prep Time: 10 minutes
Cook Time: 35 minutes

*O*live oil may be stored, unopened, on the pantry shelf for one month. Refrigerate after opening or for longer storage.

Ham & Pasta Skillet

    1 can (10 3/4 ounces) CAMPBELL'S condensed Broccoli Cheese Soup
    1 cup milk
    1 tablespoon spicy-brown mustard
    2 cups broccoli flowerets *or* 1 package (10 ounces) frozen
        broccoli cuts (2 cups)
 1 1/2 cups cooked ham strips
    3 cups cooked medium shell macaroni (about 2 cups dry)

- In medium skillet mix soup, milk, mustard and broccoli. Over medium heat, heat to a boil. Reduce heat to low. Cook 5 minutes or until broccoli is tender. Add ham and macaroni. Heat through.

Serves 4
Prep Time: 10 minutes
Cook Time: 15 minutes

Autumn Pork Chops

    1 tablespoon vegetable oil
    4 pork chops, 3/4 inch thick (about 1 1/2 pounds)
    1 can (10 3/4 ounces) CAMPBELL'S condensed Cream of Celery Soup
 1/2 cup apple juice *or* water
    2 tablespoons spicy-brown mustard
    1 tablespoon honey
      Generous dash pepper
    4 cups hot cooked medium egg noodles (about 4 cups dry)

- In medium skillet over medium-high heat, heat oil. Add chops and cook 10 minutes or until browned. Set chops aside. Pour off fat.
- Add soup, apple juice, mustard, honey and pepper. Heat to a boil. Return chops to pan. Reduce heat to low. Cover and cook 10 minutes or until chops are no longer pink. Serve with noodles.

Serves 4
Prep Time: 5 minutes
Cook Time: 25 minutes

To trim fresh broccoli into flowerets, remove large outer leaves and trim off tough parts and ends of stalks. Cut top part of stalks into small clusters.

Ham & Pasta Skillet

HARVEST PORK ROAST

    2 tablespoons vegetable oil
    3 1/2-to 4-pound boneless pork shoulder roast, netted or tied
         (Boston butt)
    1 can (10 3/4 ounces) CAMPBELL'S condensed Cream of Mushroom Soup
 1 1/4 cups water
    1 pouch CAMPBELL'S Dry Onion Soup and Recipe Mix
    1 teaspoon dried thyme leaves, crushed
    1 bay leaf
   15 small new potatoes (about 1 1/2 pounds)
  3/4 pound baby squash and/or baby carrots
    2 tablespoons all-purpose flour

- In oven-safe Dutch oven over medium-high heat, heat oil. Add roast and cook until browned. Pour off fat.

- Add mushroom soup, *1 cup water*, soup mix, thyme and bay leaf. Cover and bake at 350° F. for 45 minutes.

- Add potatoes. Cover and bake 1 hour 20 minutes. Add squash. Cover and bake 25 minutes more or until roast is fork-tender.

- Remove roast and vegetables to platter. Remove netting or string from roast. In cup mix flour and remaining water until smooth. Add gradually to soup mixture. Over medium heat, cook until mixture boils and thickens, stirring constantly. Discard bay leaf. Serve with roast and vegetables.

Serves 8
Prep Time: 5 minutes
Cook Time: 2 hours 45 minutes

Tip: Substitute 8 medium potatoes (about 3 1/2 pounds), cut into quarters and 8 medium carrots (about 1 1/4 pounds), cut into 2-inch pieces for small new potatoes, baby squash and carrots. In third step add potatoes and carrots. Cover and bake 1 hour 45 minutes more or until roast is fork-tender.

Savory Beef Roast: Substitute 3 1/2-to 4-pound boneless beef bottom round *or* chuck pot roast for pork shoulder roast. Substitute 8 medium potatoes (about 3 1/2 pounds), cut into quarters and 8 medium carrots (about 1 1/4 pounds), cut into 2-inch pieces for small new potatoes, baby squash and carrots. In third step add potatoes and carrots. Cover and bake 1 hour 45 minutes more or until roast is fork-tender.

While making the gravy, keep the meat warm by covering it lightly with foil. The roast will be easier to carve when it's had time to stand about 10 minutes.

ZESTY BAKED PORK CHOPS

- **6 pork chops, ³⁄₄ inch thick (about 2 pounds)**
- **1 can (11 ¹⁄₈ ounces) CAMPBELL'S condensed Italian Tomato Soup**
- **1 tablespoon water**
- **1 tablespoon vinegar**
- **1 tablespoon Worcestershire sauce**
- **1 tablespoon packed brown sugar**
- **¹⁄₄ to ¹⁄₂ teaspoon hot pepper sauce**

- Place chops in 3-quart shallow baking dish and bake at 400°F. for 20 minutes. Spoon off fat.
- Mix soup, water, vinegar, Worcestershire, sugar and hot pepper sauce. Spoon over chops and bake 15 minutes more or until chops are no longer pink. Remove chops. Stir sauce. If desired, garnish with *fresh oregano.*

Serves 6
Prep Time: 5 minutes
Cook Time: 35 minutes

ONION-GLORIFIED PORK CHOPS

- **2 tablespoons vegetable oil**
- **6 pork chops, ¹⁄₂ inch thick (about 1 ¹⁄₂ pounds)**
- **1 medium onion, sliced (about ¹⁄₂ cup)**
- **1 can (10 ³⁄₄ ounces) CAMPBELL'S condensed Cream of Celery Soup**
- **¹⁄₄ cup water**

- In medium skillet over medium-high heat, heat *half* the oil. Add chops in 2 batches and cook 10 minutes or until browned. Set chops aside.
- Reduce heat to medium. Add remaining oil. Add onion and cook until tender-crisp. Pour off fat.
- Add soup and water. Heat to a boil. Return chops to pan. Reduce heat to low. Cover and cook 5 minutes or until chops are no longer pink.

Serves 6
Prep Time: 5 minutes
Cook Time: 35 minutes

Zesty Baked Pork Chops

*Q*uality and quickness go hand in hand with this tasty fish and seafood selection. Recipes like *Baked Flounder Rolls, Cajun Fish and Shrimp & Broccoli* add a touch of elegance to an everyday meal or shine as the star at a special dinner with friends. Why wait for the "right" occasion? Most fish and seafood takes just minutes to cook, and CAMPBELL'S Soups make preparation even easier. *Cheesy Tuna & Noodles,* a real family-pleaser, is a shortcut version of the traditional tuna noodle casserole: It's ready in only 30 minutes! With these great-tasting recipes you'll experience the full flavor of the sea without setting sail!

Fish with Lemon Dill Sauce, top, (page 90) and Oriental Shrimp Kabobs, bottom, (page 92).

BAKED FLOUNDER ROLLS

1   can (10 3/4 ounces) **CAMPBELL'S** condensed Cream of Mushroom Soup
1/4 cup milk
3   tablespoons lemon juice
1/4 teaspoon dried dill weed, crushed
3   cups hot cooked rice
4   fresh *or* thawed frozen flounder *or* other firm white fish fillets
1   package (about 10 ounces) frozen broccoli spears, thawed and drained
3   tablespoons sliced almonds

- Mix soup, milk, *2 tablespoons* lemon juice and dill. Mix *1/2 cup* soup mixture and rice in 2-quart shallow baking dish. Set aside.
- Sprinkle remaining lemon juice over fillets. Divide broccoli spears among fillets and roll up like a jelly roll. Arrange seam-side down over rice mixture.
- Spoon remaining soup mixture over roll-ups. Sprinkle almonds and *1/8 teaspoon paprika* over soup mixture.
- Bake at 400° F. for 20 minutes or until fish flakes easily when tested with a fork.

Serves 4
Prep Time: 20 minutes
Cook Time: 20 minutes

FISH WITH LEMON DILL SAUCE

1   can (10 3/4 ounces) **CAMPBELL'S** condensed Cream of Celery Soup
2   tablespoons water
1   teaspoon prepared mustard
1/2 teaspoon dried dill weed, crushed
1   pound fresh *or* thawed frozen firm white fish fillets (cod, haddock *or* halibut)
4   thin lemon slices

- In medium skillet mix soup, water, mustard and dill. Over medium heat, heat to a boil. Arrange fish in soup mixture. Top with lemon slices.
- Reduce heat to low. Cover and cook 10 minutes or until fish flakes easily when tested with a fork. If desired, serve with sauce and *hot cooked rice*; garnish with *lemon* and *fresh dill*.

Serves 4
Prep Time: 5 minutes
Cook Time: 15 minutes

Baked Flounder Rolls

QUICK CLAMS & PASTA

1 can (10¾ ounces) CAMPBELL'S condensed New England Clam Chowder
½ **cup milk**
¼ **teaspoon garlic powder**
⅛ **teaspoon pepper**
2 **cups hot cooked spaghetti (about 4 ounces dry)**

- In medium saucepan mix soup, milk, garlic powder and pepper. Over low heat, heat through, stirring occasionally. Serve over spaghetti. If desired, garnish with *fresh parsley*.

Serves 2
Prep Time: 10 minutes
Cook Time: 10 minutes

*C*urly leaf parsley and Italian parsely, also known as flat leaf, are the two main varieties of parsley grown in the U.S.

ORIENTAL SHRIMP KABOBS

1 can (10¾ ounces) CAMPBELL'S condensed Tomato Soup
¼ **cup orange juice**
1 **tablespoon soy sauce**
1 **tablespoon vegetable oil**
¼ **teaspoon ground ginger**
1½ **pounds large shrimp, shelled and deveined**

- Mix soup, orange juice, soy, oil and ginger in large shallow nonmetallic dish. Add shrimp and toss to coat. Cover and refrigerate 1 hour.
- Remove shrimp from marinade. On 6 long skewers, thread shrimp.
- Place kabobs on lightly oiled grill rack over medium coals. Grill uncovered 10 minutes or until shrimp turn pink, turning and brushing often with marinade.
- Heat remaining marinade to a boil and serve with shrimp.

Serves 6
Prep Time: 20 minutes
Marinating Time: 1 hour
Cook Time: 10 minutes

Quick Clams & Pasta

CHEESY TUNA & NOODLES

Canned tuna comes in several varieties. Solid or fancy tuna consists of large chunks. Chunk tuna has slightly smaller pieces. Flaked or grated tuna works best for sandwiches and is the least expensive.

3 packages (3 ounces *each*) CAMPBELL'S or SANWA RAMEN PRIDE Chicken Flavor Ramen Noodle Soup
1 can (10¾ ounces) CAMPBELL'S condensed Cream of Mushroom Soup
¾ cup milk
⅛ teaspoon garlic powder
⅛ teaspoon pepper
1 package (about 9 ounces) frozen mixed vegetables (about 2 cups), thawed and drained
1½ cups shredded mozzarella cheese (6 ounces)
1 can (about 6 ounces) tuna, drained and flaked

- Cook noodles according to package directions. Stir in seasoning packets. Drain off most of liquid. Set aside.
- In medium skillet mix mushroom soup, milk, garlic powder, pepper and vegetables. Over medium heat, heat to a boil. Reduce heat to low. Cover and cook 5 minutes or until vegetables are tender, stirring occasionally. Add cheese and cook until cheese is melted, stirring occasionally.
- Add tuna and reserved noodles. Heat through, stirring occasionally. If desired, garnish with *fresh parsley*.

Serves 6
Prep Time: 10 minutes
Cook Time: 20 minutes

Tip: To thaw vegetables, microwave on HIGH 4 minutes.

Salmon Noodle Skillet: Substitute 1 package (about 10 ounces) frozen cut green beans (about 2 cups), thawed and drained for mixed vegetables. In second step add green beans and 1 can (8 ounces) sliced water chestnuts, drained with soup. Substitute 1 can (about 8 ounces) salmon for tuna.

Shrimp is cooked when the flesh turns opaque. Be careful not to overcook shellfish or its texture will be tough and rubbery.

SHRIMP & CORN CREOLE

2 tablespoons margarine *or* butter
½ teaspoon dried oregano leaves, crushed
½ teaspoon paprika
¼ teaspoon garlic powder *or* 2 cloves garlic, minced
¼ teaspoon black pepper
¼ teaspoon ground red pepper
1 can (10 ¾ ounces) **CAMPBELL'S** condensed Golden Corn Soup
1 can (about 14 ½ ounces) stewed tomatoes
1 pound medium shrimp, shelled and deveined
4 cups hot cooked rice

- In medium skillet over medium heat, heat margarine. Add oregano, paprika, garlic powder, black pepper and red pepper and cook 1 minute, stirring constantly.
- Add soup and tomatoes. Heat to a boil. Reduce heat to low. Cook 5 minutes.
- Add shrimp. Cook 5 minutes or until shrimp turn pink, stirring often. Serve over rice. If desired, garnish with *fresh oregano* and *parsley*.

Serves 4
Prep Time: 15 minutes
Cook Time: 20 minutes

SHRIMP & BROCCOLI

1 tablespoon olive *or* vegetable oil
2 cups broccoli flowerets
¼ teaspoon garlic powder *or* 2 cloves garlic, minced
1 can (10 ¾ ounces) **CAMPBELL'S** condensed Cream of Broccoli Soup
½ cup water
1 tablespoon lemon juice
⅛ teaspoon pepper
1 pound medium shrimp, shelled and deveined
4 cups hot cooked rice

- In medium skillet over medium heat, heat oil. Add broccoli and garlic powder and cook until tender-crisp. Add soup, water, lemon juice and pepper. Heat to a boil. Add shrimp. Reduce heat to low. Cook 5 minutes or until shrimp turn pink, stirring often. Serve over rice.

Serves 4
Prep Time: 20 minutes
Cook Time: 15 minutes

Shrimp & Corn Creole

Cajun Fish

1 tablespoon vegetable oil
1 small green pepper, diced (about ⅔ cup)
½ teaspoon dried oregano leaves, crushed
1 can (10¾ ounces) CAMPBELL'S condensed Tomato Soup
⅓ cup water
⅛ teaspoon garlic powder
⅛ teaspoon black pepper
⅛ teaspoon ground red pepper
1 pound fresh *or* thawed frozen firm white fish fillets (cod, haddock *or* halibut)

- In medium skillet over medium heat, heat oil. Add green pepper and oregano and cook until tender-crisp, stirring often. Add soup, water, garlic powder, black pepper and red pepper. Heat to a boil.
- Place fish in soup mixture. Reduce heat to low. Cover and cook 5 minutes or until fish flakes easily when tested with a fork. Serve with *parslied rice*. If desired, garnish with *fresh thyme*.

Serves 4
Prep Time: 10 minutes
Cook Time: 15 minutes

Broccoli Fish Bake

1 package (about 10 ounces) frozen broccoli spears, cooked and drained *or* 1 pound fresh broccoli, cut into spears, cooked and drained
1 pound fresh *or* thawed frozen firm white fish fillets (cod, haddock *or* halibut)
1 can (10¾ ounces) CAMPBELL'S HEALTHY REQUEST condensed Cream of Broccoli Soup
⅓ cup milk
¼ cup shredded Cheddar cheese (1 ounce)
2 tablespoons dry bread crumbs
1 teaspoon margarine, melted

- In 2-quart shallow baking dish arrange broccoli. Top with fish. Mix soup and milk and pour over fish.
- Sprinkle cheese over soup mixture. Mix bread crumbs, margarine and ⅛ *teaspoon paprika* and sprinkle over cheese. Bake at 450° F. for 20 minutes or until fish flakes easily when tested with a fork.

Serves 4
Prep Time: 15 minutes
Cook Time: 20 minutes

It is recommended that fish be stored in the coldest section of the refrigerator for only one day. In the freezer, fish may be stored for three to six months.

Cajun Fish

*A*s a delicious all-in-one meal or a sensational side dish, these great-tasting pasta and rice recipes are sure to please family and friends. Bursting with flavor, main-dish *Pasta Primavera, Spaghetti Florentine* or *Baked Macaroni & Cheese* double as side dish accompaniments for chicken, steak or pork when served in smaller portions. For a ready-in-a-flash tasty side dish on busy nights, *Mushroom Broccoli Alfredo, Fiesta Tomato Rice* and *Souper-Quick Southwestern Rice* provide all-family appeal. These fuss-free favorites are sure to get the cook out of the kitchen — fast!

Baked Macaroni & Cheese, left, (page 111) and Pasta Primavera, right, (page 105).

*C*hoose firm bulbs of garlic with dry, unbroken skins. Avoid bulbs with soft, shriveled or sprouting cloves.

*S*PAGHETTI FLORENTINE

Vegetable cooking spray
1 **medium onion, chopped (about** $1/2$ **cup)**
3 **cloves garlic, minced**
1 **teaspoon Italian seasoning, crushed**
1 **can (10** $3/4$ **ounces) CAMPBELL'S HEALTHY REQUEST condensed Cream of Celery Soup**
$1/8$ **teaspoon pepper**
1 **package (about 10 ounces) frozen chopped spinach**
1 **cup plain yogurt**
1 **medium tomato, diced (about 1 cup)**
4 **cups hot cooked spaghetti (about 8 ounces dry)**
Parmesan cheese

- Spray medium saucepan with cooking spray and heat over medium heat 1 minute. Add onion, garlic and Italian seasoning and cook until tender, stirring often.
- Add soup, pepper and spinach. Heat to a boil. Reduce heat to low. Cover and cook 10 minutes or until spinach is tender, breaking apart spinach with fork and stirring occasionally.
- Add yogurt and tomato and heat through. Toss with spaghetti. Sprinkle with cheese. If desired, garnish with *fresh basil.*

Serves 4
Prep Time: 10 minutes
Cook Time: 25 minutes

*Q*UICK SEASONED POTATOES

1 **can (14** $1/2$ **ounces) SWANSON Chicken Broth**
Generous dash pepper
$1 1/3$ **cups instant mashed potato flakes *or* buds**

- In medium saucepan over medium-high heat, heat broth and pepper to a boil. Stir in potato flakes until liquid is absorbed.

Serves 4
Prep Time: 5 minutes
Cook Time: 5 minutes

Spaghetti Florentine

*B*rowning the rice in oil helps keep the grains separate and imparts a wonderful nutty flavor to this tasty side dish.

*F*IESTA TOMATO RICE

> 1 tablespoon vegetable oil
> 1 large onion, chopped (about 1 cup)
> 1 large green pepper, chopped (about 1 cup)
> 1/8 teaspoon garlic powder *or* 1 clove garlic, minced
> 1 cup uncooked regular long-grain rice
> 1 can (11 1/8 ounces) **CAMPBELL'S** condensed Fiesta Tomato Soup
> 2 cups water

- In large saucepan over medium heat, heat oil. Add onion, pepper and garlic powder. Cook until tender-crisp.
- Add rice and cook 30 seconds, stirring constantly. Stir in soup and water. Heat to a boil. Reduce heat to low. Cover and cook 25 minutes or until rice is done and most of liquid is absorbed.

Serves 4
Prep Time: 10 minutes
Cook Time: 35 minutes

PASTA PRIMAVERA

    2 tablespoons cornstarch
    I can (10 ½ ounces) CAMPBELL'S condensed Chicken Broth
    ½ cup water
    I teaspoon dried basil leaves, crushed
    ¼ teaspoon garlic powder *or* 2 cloves garlic, minced
    2 cups broccoli flowerets
    2 medium carrots, sliced (about I cup)
    I medium onion, cut into wedges
    I medium tomato, diced (about I cup)
    4 cups hot cooked thin spaghetti (about 8 ounces dry)
       Grated Parmesan cheese

- In cup mix cornstarch and *¾ cup* broth until smooth. Set aside.
- In large saucepan mix remaining broth, water, basil, garlic powder, broccoli, carrots and onion. Over medium-high heat, heat to a boil. Reduce heat to low. Cover and cook 5 minutes or until vegetables are tender.
- Stir cornstarch mixture and add. Cook until mixture boils and thickens, stirring constantly. Stir in tomato. Toss with spaghetti. Serve with cheese.

Serves 4
Prep Time: 15 minutes
Cook Time: 15 minutes

Store tomatoes, *unwashed,* at room temperature, with stem end down, until slightly soft and ripe. Ripened tomatoes may be refrigerated for up to four days.

SHORTCUT RISOTTO

    I tablespoon margarine *or* butter
    I medium onion, chopped (about ½ cup)
    I cup uncooked regular long-grain rice
    I can (10 ½ ounces) CAMPBELL'S condensed Chicken Broth
    I soup can water
    3 tablespoons grated Parmesan cheese

- In medium saucepan over medium heat, heat margarine. Add onion and cook until tender-crisp.
- Add rice and cook 30 seconds, stirring constantly. Stir in broth and water. Heat to a boil. Reduce heat to low. Cover and cook 20 minutes or until rice is done and most of liquid is absorbed.
- Stir in cheese.

Serves 4
Prep Time: 10 minutes
Cook Time: 30 minutes

*V*EGETABLE STUFFING BAKE

4 cups **PEPPERIDGE FARM** Herb Seasoned Stuffing
2 tablespoons margarine *or* butter, melted
1 can (10 ¾ ounces) **CAMPBELL'S** condensed Cream of Mushroom Soup
½ cup sour cream
2 small zucchini, shredded (about 2 cups)
2 medium carrots, shredded (about 1 cup)
1 small onion, finely chopped (about ¼ cup)

- Mix *1 cup* stuffing and margarine. Set aside.
- Mix soup, sour cream, zucchini, carrots and onion. Add remaining stuffing. Mix lightly. Spoon into 1½-quart casserole. Sprinkle with reserved stuffing mixture.
- Bake at 350° F. for 35 minutes or until hot.

Serves 6
Prep Time: 15 minutes
Cook Time: 35 minutes

Tip: To melt margarine, remove wrapper and place in microwave-safe cup. Cover and microwave on HIGH 30 seconds.

*M*EXICAN CHEESE CORN BREAD

1 can (10 ¾ ounces) **CAMPBELL'S** condensed Golden Corn Soup
2 eggs
¼ cup milk
1 package (12 ounces) corn muffin mix
1 can (about 4 ounces) chopped green chilies, drained
1 cup shredded Cheddar cheese (4 ounces)

- Preheat oven to 400°F. Grease 9-inch square baking pan.
- Mix soup, eggs and milk. Stir in corn muffin mix just until blended. Fold in chilies and ½ *cup* cheese. Pour into prepared pan, spreading evenly. Sprinkle with remaining cheese.
- Bake 20 minutes or until toothpick inserted in center comes out clean.

Serves 12
Prep Time: 10 minutes
Cook Time: 20 minutes

Hard cheeses such as Parmesan and Romano are typically grated; 2 ounces of hard cheese will yield about ½ cup grated.

BROCCOLI & NOODLES SUPREME

- **3 cups dry medium egg noodles**
- **2 cups fresh *or* frozen broccoli flowerets**
- **1 can (10¾ ounces) CAMPBELL'S condensed Cream of Chicken & Broccoli Soup**
- **½ cup sour cream**
- **⅛ teaspoon pepper**
- **⅓ cup grated Parmesan cheese**

- In large saucepan prepare noodles according to package directions. Add broccoli for last 5 minutes of cooking time. Drain in colander.
- In same pan mix soup, sour cream, pepper, cheese and noodle mixture. Heat through, stirring occasionally. If desired, garnish with *red pepper*, *carrot* and *fresh parsley*.

Serves 5
Prep Time: 5 minutes
Cook Time: 20 minutes

MUSHROOM BROCCOLI ALFREDO

2 tablespoons margarine *or* butter, melted
3 cups broccoli flowerets
3 cups sliced mushrooms (about 8 ounces)
1 medium onion, coarsely chopped (about ½ cup)
¼ teaspoon garlic powder or 2 cloves garlic, minced
1 can (10¾ ounces) CAMPBELL'S condensed Cream of Mushroom Soup
⅓ cup milk
⅛ teaspoon pepper
2 tablespoons grated Parmesan cheese
4 cups hot cooked fettuccine *or* spaghetti (about 8 ounces dry)

- In medium skillet over medium heat, heat margarine. Add broccoli, mushrooms, onion and garlic powder. Cook until tender-crisp.
- Add soup, milk, pepper and cheese. Heat through, stirring occasionally. Serve over fettuccine. If desired, garnish with additional *Parmesan cheese*.

Serves 4
Prep Time: 15 minutes
Cook Time: 15 minutes

Tip: Substitute ⅓ cup Chablis *or* other dry white wine for milk.

*I*nstant rice
has been fully or
partially cooked,
then dehydrated
so it only takes
a few minutes
to cook.

*S*OUPER-QUICK SOUTHWESTERN RICE

**I can (10¾ ounces) CAMPBELL'S condensed
Southwestern-Style Chicken Vegetable Soup**
I cup water
1¼ cups uncooked instant rice

- In medium saucepan mix soup and water. Over medium-high heat,
  heat to a boil.
- Stir in rice. Cover and remove from heat. Let stand 5 minutes.
  Fluff with fork.

Serves 3
Prep Time: 5 minutes
Cook Time: 5 minutes
Stand Time: 5 minutes

BAKED MACARONI & CHEESE

- 2 cans (10 ¾ ounces *each*) **CAMPBELL'S** condensed **Cheddar Cheese Soup**
- 1 soup can milk
- ¼ teaspoon pepper
- 4 cups hot cooked medium shell *or* corkscrew macaroni (about 3 cups dry)
- 2 tablespoons dry bread crumbs
- 1 tablespoon margarine *or* butter, melted

- In 2-quart casserole mix soup, milk, pepper and macaroni.
- Mix bread crumbs with margarine and sprinkle over macaroni mixture.
- Bake at 400° F. for 25 minutes or until hot.

Serves 8
Prep Time: 20 minutes
Cook Time: 25 minutes

Tip: Recipe may be halved. Halve all ingredients, except decrease margarine to 2 teaspoons, use 1-quart casserole and decrease baking time to 20 minutes.

SOUPER RICE

- 1 can (10 ½ ounces) **CAMPBELL'S** condensed **Vegetable Soup**
- 1 ½ soup cans water
- 1 cup uncooked regular long-grain rice

- In medium saucepan mix soup and water. Over medium heat, heat to a boil. Stir in rice. Reduce heat to low. Cover and cook 20 minutes or until rice is done and most of liquid is absorbed, stirring occasionally.

Serves 4
Prep Time: 5 minutes
Cook Time: 25 minutes

To melt 1 tablespoon margarine or butter quickly, remove wrapper and place in microwave-safe cup. Cover and microwave on HIGH about 30 seconds.

*F*eatured here are some of CAMPBELL'S pick-of-the-crop vegetable combinations and salads! *Vegetable Rotini, Cheddar Potato Slices* and *Glazed Vegetables* make flavorful companions for a variety of entrées. And remember, popular *Green Bean Bake,* a CAMPBELL'S favorite since its creation in 1955; it's the perfect casserole for potlucks and family suppers. For patio, picnic or buffet fare, this selection of main dish and side dish salads is ideal whatever the occasion. Use this wide array of tasty vegetables and salads to turn the kitchen rush hour into a relaxing ride!

Clockwise from far right: Cheddar Potato Slices (page 117), Green Bean Bake (page 121) and Vegetable Rotini (page 114).

CREAMY VEGETABLE MEDLEY

- 1 can (10 3/4 ounces) CAMPBELL'S condensed Cream of Celery Soup
- 1/2 cup milk
- 2 cups broccoli flowerets
- 2 medium carrots, sliced (about 1 cup)
- 1 cup cauliflower flowerets

- In medium saucepan mix soup, milk, broccoli, carrots and cauliflower. Over medium heat, heat to a boil.
- Reduce heat to low. Cover and cook 15 minutes or until vegetables are tender, stirring occasionally.

Serves 6
Prep Time: 15 minutes
Cook Time: 20 minutes

VEGETABLE ROTINI

- 2 1/2 cups dry corkscrew macaroni
- 1 1/2 cups fresh *or* frozen broccoli flowerets
- 1 1/2 cups fresh *or* frozen cauliflower flowerets
- 2 medium carrots, cut into 2-inch matchstick-thin strips (about 1 cup)
- 1 package (3 ounces) cream cheese *or* cream cheese with chives, softened
- 1 can (10 3/4 ounces) CAMPBELL'S condensed Broccoli Cheese Soup
- 3/4 cup milk
- 2 tablespoons Dijon-style mustard (optional)
- 1/8 teaspoon pepper
- 1/2 cup grated Parmesan cheese

- In large saucepan prepare macaroni according to package directions. Add broccoli, cauliflower and carrots for last 5 minutes of cooking time. Drain in colander.
- In same pan stir cream cheese until smooth. Stir in soup, milk, mustard, pepper and Parmesan cheese. Over low heat, heat through. Add macaroni mixture and heat through, stirring occasionally. If desired, garnish with *fresh basil*.

Serves 6
Prep Time: 15 minutes
Cook Time: 20 minutes

Tip: To soften cream cheese, remove wrapper. On microwave-safe plate, microwave on HIGH 10 seconds.

Creamy Vegetable Medley

*T*wo cans
(5 ounces *each*)
SWANSON
Premium Chunk
Chicken, drained,
will yield the
2 cups cubed
cooked chicken
needed for this
recipe.

*C*HICKEN 'N' TWISTS

  1 can (10 1/2 ounces) **CAMPBELL'S** condensed Chicken Broth
1/4 cup milk *or* water
1/2 cup mayonnaise
1/4 cup grated Parmesan cheese
  1 teaspoon dried basil leaves, crushed
  3 cups hot cooked corkscrew macaroni (about 2 1/2 cups dry)
  1 cup cherry tomatoes cut in half
  1 cup frozen peas
1/2 cup sliced mushrooms (about 2 ounces)
  1 small red onion, chopped (about 1/4 cup)
  2 cups cubed cooked chicken
    Salad greens

- In medium bowl mix broth, milk, mayonnaise, cheese and basil.
- In large shallow nonmetallic dish toss macaroni, tomatoes, peas, mushrooms, onion, chicken and broth mixture until evenly coated. Refrigerate at least 4 hours. Serve on salad greens.

Serves 4
Prep Time: 20 minutes
Chill Time: 4 hours

CHEDDAR POTATO SLICES

- 1 can (10¾ ounces) CAMPBELL'S condensed **Cream of Mushroom Soup**
- ½ teaspoon paprika
- ½ teaspoon pepper
- 4 medium baking potatoes (about 1¼ pounds), sliced ¼ inch thick
- 1 cup shredded **Cheddar cheese** (4 ounces)

- Mix soup, paprika and pepper. In greased 2-quart shallow baking dish arrange potatoes in overlapping rows. Sprinkle with cheese. Spoon soup mixture over cheese.
- Cover and bake at 400° F. for 45 minutes. Uncover and bake 10 minutes more or until potatoes are tender. If desired, garnish with *fresh parsley*.

Serves 6
Prep Time: 15 minutes
Cook Time: 55 minutes

GLAZED VEGETABLES

- 2 tablespoons cornstarch
- 1 can (14½ ounces) SWANSON **Vegetable Broth**
- ½ teaspoon ground ginger
- ¼ teaspoon garlic powder *or* 2 cloves garlic, minced
- 2 medium carrots, sliced (about 1 cup)
- 2 stalks celery, sliced (about 1 cup)
- 1 small green *or* red pepper, cut into 2-inch-long strips (about 1 cup)
- 1 large onion, cut into wedges
- 1 cup fresh *or* frozen broccoli flowerets
- 4 ounces snow peas

- In cup mix together cornstarch and ¼ *cup* broth until smooth. Set aside.
- In medium skillet mix remaining broth, ginger, garlic powder, carrots, celery, pepper, onion, broccoli and snow peas. Over medium-high heat, heat to a boil. Reduce heat to medium. Cover and cook 5 minutes or until vegetables are tender.
- Stir cornstarch mixture and add. Cook until mixture boils and thickens, stirring constantly.

Serves 4
Prep Time: 15 minutes
Cook Time: 15 minutes

Choose potatoes that are firm, well-shaped and free from blemishes or sprouts. Avoid soft, green, shriveled or blemished potatoes.

GRILLED CHICKEN SALAD

    1   can (10 3/4 ounces) CAMPBELL'S condensed Tomato Soup
    1   tablespoon soy sauce
    1   tablespoon vinegar
  1/4   teaspoon ground ginger
  1/8   teaspoon garlic powder *or* 1 clove garlic, minced
    4   skinless, boneless chicken breast halves (about 1 pound)
    8   cups salad greens torn in bite-size pieces

- Mix soup, soy, vinegar, ginger and garlic powder.
- Place chicken on lightly oiled grill rack over medium-hot coals. Grill uncovered 15 minutes or until chicken is no longer pink, turning and brushing often with soup mixture. Slice chicken into thin strips.
- Heat remaining soup mixture to a boil. Arrange salad greens on platter. Arrange chicken over salad greens. Spoon soup mixture over chicken.

Serves 4
Prep Time: 10 minutes
Cook Time: 15 minutes

Broiled Chicken Salad: Prepare as in first step. Place chicken on rack in broiler pan. Broil 4 inches from heat 15 minutes or until chicken is no longer pink, turning and brushing often with soup mixture. Proceed as in third step.

Select salad greens with tender leaves free of blemishes and brown, moist residue. Avoid bunches with thick, coarsely-veined leaves.

Cabbage is hearty and can be stored up to two weeks in the refrigerator in a plastic bag. When preparing, tear off any wilted outer leaves, rinse and halve lengthwise to remove core.

SHORTCUT COLESLAW

| | 1 | can (10 ¾ ounces) **CAMPBELL'S** condensed Cream of Celery Soup |

1   can (10¾ ounces) **CAMPBELL'S** condensed Cream of Celery Soup
⅓   cup mayonnaise
⅓   cup cider vinegar
2   tablespoons sugar
1   tablespoon prepared mustard
1   teaspoon celery seed (optional)
½   teaspoon pepper
2   packages (16 ounces *each*) coleslaw mix

- In small bowl mix soup, mayonnaise, vinegar, sugar, mustard, celery seed and pepper.
- In large bowl toss coleslaw mix and soup mixture until evenly coated. Refrigerate at least 2 hours. If desired, garnish with *celery leaves* and *fresh parsley*.

Serves 16
Prep Time: 10 minutes
Chill Time: 2 hours

Tip: Substitute 1 small head cabbage, shredded (about 5 cups) and 2 medium carrots, shredded (about 1 cup) for coleslaw mix.

*G*REEN BEAN BAKE

  1 can (10¾ ounces) CAMPBELL'S condensed Cream of Mushroom Soup
 ½ cup milk
  1 teaspoon soy sauce
     Dash pepper
  4 cups cooked cut green beans
  1 can (2.8 ounces) French fried onions

- In 1½-quart casserole mix soup, milk, soy, pepper, beans and ½ *can* onions.
- Bake at 350° F. for 25 minutes or until hot.
- Stir. Sprinkle remaining onions over bean mixture. Bake 5 minutes more or until onions are golden.

Serves 6
Prep Time: 10 minutes
Cook Time: 30 minutes

Green Bean Bake Italiano: Substitute 4 cups cooked Italian green beans for green beans. In third step, before topping with remaining onions, top casserole with 1 small tomato, chopped (about ½ cup) and sprinkle with ⅛ teaspoon *each* dried oregano and basil leaves, crushed.

*T*OMATO-ZUCCHINI MEDLEY

  1 can (10¾ ounces) CAMPBELL'S condensed Tomato Soup
  1 tablespoon lemon juice
 ½ teaspoon dried basil leaves, crushed
 ½ teaspoon garlic powder
  4 medium zucchini, sliced (about 6 cups)
  1 small green pepper, cut into 2-inch-long strips (about 1 cup)
  1 large onion, sliced (about 1 cup)
 ¼ cup grated Parmesan cheese

- In Dutch oven mix soup, lemon juice, basil, garlic powder, zucchini, pepper and onion. Over medium heat, heat to a boil.
- Reduce heat to low. Cover and cook 15 minutes or until vegetables are tender, stirring occasionally. Stir in cheese.

Serves 8
Prep Time: 15 minutes
Cook Time: 25 minutes

*F*or 4 cups cooked green beans, choose from either 1 bag (16-20 ounces) frozen cut green beans, 2 cans (about 16 ounces *each*) cut green beans, drained or about 1½ pounds fresh green beans.

$\mathcal{M}$ARINATED VEGETABLES

- 1 can (14 ½ ounces) SWANSON Vegetable Broth
- 1 tablespoon sugar
- ½ teaspoon dried thyme leaves, crushed
- ¼ teaspoon garlic powder *or* 2 cloves garlic, minced
- ⅛ teaspoon pepper
- 4 cups cauliflower flowerets (about 1 small head)
- ½ pound green beans, cut into 1-inch pieces (about 1 ½ cups)
- 2 medium carrots, sliced (about 1 cup)
- ¼ cup vinegar
- 2 tablespoons chopped fresh parsley *or* 2 teaspoons dried parsley flakes

- In large saucepan over high heat, heat broth, sugar, thyme, garlic powder and pepper to a boil. Add cauliflower, beans and carrots. Reduce heat to low. Cover and cook 1 minute or until vegetables are tender-crisp.
- Place vegetables and broth mixture in shallow nonmetallic dish. Add vinegar and parsley. Refrigerate at least 12 hours, stirring occasionally.
- Serve vegetables with slotted spoon.

Serves 12
Prep Time: 15 minutes
Cook Time: 10 minutes
Marinating Time: 12 hours

$\mathcal{T}$o ensure peak flavor and fresh-ness, store fresh green beans, *unwashed*, in a perforated bag and refrigerate for up to four days.

$\mathcal{P}$OTATO KABOBS WITH CHEESE SAUCE

- 6 medium baking potatoes (about 2 pounds)
- 2 tablespoons vegetable oil
- 1 can (10¾ ounces) CAMPBELL'S condensed Cheddar Cheese Soup
- ⅓ cup milk

- Cut potatoes in half lengthwise. Cut each half crosswise into 4 pieces.
- On 6 long skewers, thread potatoes. Brush with oil. Place kabobs on lightly oiled grill rack over medium-hot coals. Grill uncovered 30 minutes or until potatoes are fork-tender, turning once during cooking.
- In small saucepan mix soup and milk. Over low heat, heat through, stirring often. Serve over potatoes. If desired, garnish with *fresh sage* and *parsley*.

Serves 6
Prep Time: 10 minutes
Cook Time: 30 minutes

Marinated Vegetables
(top), Potato Kabobs with
Cheese Sauce

No need to stew over what to serve for dinner. *Seafood Chowder, Spicy Vegetable Chili* and *Country Chicken Stew* are just a few of the souper suppers-in-a-bowl designed to serve a few or a hungry crowd. Whatever the occasion, your family will welcome the warmth of such full-flavored soups as *Ratatouille Soup* or *Vegetable Beef Soup.* Rely on CAMPBELL'S condensed Soups as the base for these sensational soups and stews to shorten cooking time without sacrificing flavor. Add a tossed salad and crusty bread, and these soups and stews will add a warm glow to even the chilliest night.

Tortellini Soup, left, (page 129) and Chicken Chili, right, (page 126).

Spicy Vegetable Chili

1 can (10 3/4 ounces) **CAMPBELL'S condensed Tomato Soup**
1 can (10 3/4 ounces) **CAMPBELL'S condensed Cream of Onion Soup**
2 **soup cans water**
1 **tablespoon chili powder**
1/2 **teaspoon dried thyme leaves, crushed**
1/8 **teaspoon pepper**
2 **small zucchini, coarsely chopped (about 2 cups)**
2 **medium carrots, coarsely chopped (about 1 cup)**
1 **can (about 16 ounces) chick peas (garbanzo beans),**
   rinsed and drained
1 **can (about 16 ounces) black beans, rinsed and drained**

- In large saucepan mix soups, water, chili powder, thyme, pepper, zucchini, carrots, chick peas and black beans.
- Over medium heat, heat to a boil. Reduce heat to low. Cook 40 minutes, stirring occasionally. If desired, garnish with *shredded Cheddar cheese* and *fresh parsley.*

Serves 6
Prep Time: 10 minutes
Cook Time: 45 minutes

Chicken Chili

1 **tablespoon vegetable oil**
1 **pound skinless, boneless chicken breasts,**
   cut into cubes
1 **tablespoon chili powder**
1 can (10 3/4 ounces) **CAMPBELL'S condensed Cream of Chicken Soup**
2 **cups water**
1 **pouch CAMPBELL'S Dry Onion Soup and Recipe Mix**
2 **cans (about 16 ounces *each*) white kidney (cannellini) beans,**
   rinsed and drained

- In large saucepan over medium heat, heat oil. Add chicken and chili powder and cook 5 minutes, stirring often.
- Add chicken soup, water and soup mix. Heat to a boil. Reduce heat to low. Cover and cook 10 minutes. Add beans. Heat through. If desired, garnish with *shredded Cheddar cheese* and *green onion.*

Serves 5
Prep Time: 10 minutes
Cook Time: 25 minutes

Beans are an excellent source of fiber. An easy way to reduce sodium is to rinse and drain the canned beans before adding to this recipe.

Spicy Vegetable Chili

*T*o cut turkey into cubes, first cut into strips about ½-inch wide. Line up strips; then cut crosswise into ½-inch pieces.

SMOKED TURKEY BEAN SOUP

  1 tablespoon vegetable oil
  1 medium onion, chopped (about ½ cup)
 ¼ teaspoon garlic powder *or* 2 cloves garlic, minced
  1 can (26 ounces) CAMPBELL'S condensed Cream of Chicken Soup
  3 cups water
  1 teaspoon paprika
  1 can (about 16 ounces) white kidney (cannellini) beans, rinsed and drained
  1 cup cubed smoked turkey breast *or* smoked ham
  1 tablespoon chopped fresh parsley *or* 1 teaspoon dried parsley flakes

- In large saucepan over medium heat, heat oil. Add onion and garlic powder and cook until tender, stirring occasionally.
- Add soup, water and paprika. Heat to a boil. Reduce heat to low. Cook 5 minutes, stirring occasionally. Add beans, turkey and parsley. Heat through. If desired, sprinkle with additional *paprika*.

Serves 6
Prep Time: 10 minutes
Cook Time: 20 minutes

$\mathcal{T}$ORTELLINI SOUP

  2 cans (14 $^1\!/_2$ ounces *each*) **SWANSON NATURAL GOODNESS
      Chicken Broth**
$^1\!/_8$ teaspoon pepper
  1 medium carrot, sliced (about $^1\!/_2$ cup)
  1 stalk celery, sliced (about $^1\!/_2$ cup)
  2 ounces frozen cheese-filled tortellini (about $^1\!/_2$ cup)
  1 tablespoon chopped fresh parsley *or* 1 teaspoon dried parsley flakes

- In medium saucepan mix broth, pepper, carrot and celery. Over medium-high heat, heat to a boil. Add tortellini. Reduce heat to medium. Cook 15 minutes or until tortellini is done, stirring occasionally. Stir in parsley.

Serves 4
Prep Time: 10 minutes
Cook Time: 20 minutes

$\mathcal{H}$OME-STYLE BEEF STEW

  2 tablespoons all-purpose flour
$^1\!/_8$ teaspoon pepper
  1 pound beef for stew, cut into 1-inch cubes
  1 tablespoon vegetable oil
  1 can (10 $^1\!/_2$ ounces) **CAMPBELL'S condensed Beef Broth**
$^1\!/_2$ cup water
$^1\!/_2$ teaspoon dried thyme leaves, crushed
  1 bay leaf
  3 medium carrots (about $^1\!/_2$ pound), cut into 1-inch pieces
  2 medium potatoes (about $^1\!/_2$ pound), cut into quarters

- Mix flour and pepper on plate. Coat beef with flour mixture.
- In Dutch oven over medium-high heat, heat oil. Add beef and cook until browned, stirring often. Set beef aside. Pour off fat.
- Add broth, water, thyme and bay leaf. Heat to a boil. Return beef to pan. Reduce heat to low. Cover and cook 1 $^1\!/_2$ hours.
- Add carrots and potatoes. Cover and cook 30 minutes more or until beef is fork-tender, stirring occasionally. Discard bay leaf.

Serves 4
Prep Time: 10 minutes
Cook Time: 2 hours 15 minutes

$\mathcal{T}$ortellini is a type of stuffed pasta. The pasta dough is cut into triangles, topped with a meat or cheese filling, folded over and then shaped into small rings.

COUNTRY CHICKEN STEW

- 2 tablespoons margarine *or* butter
- 1 medium onion, sliced (about ½ cup)
- 1 can (10¾ ounces) **CAMPBELL'S condensed Cream of Chicken Soup**
- 1 soup can water
- ½ teaspoon dried oregano leaves, crushed
- 3 medium potatoes, cut into 1-inch pieces (about 3 cups)
- 2 medium carrots, sliced (about 1 cup)
- 1 cup frozen cut green beans
- 2 cups cubed cooked chicken
- 2 tablespoons chopped fresh parsley
- 2 slices bacon, cooked and crumbled

- In medium skillet over medium heat, heat margarine. Add onion and cook until tender.
- Add soup, water, oregano, potatoes and carrots. Heat to a boil. Reduce heat to low. Cover and cook 15 minutes, stirring occasionally.
- Add beans. Cover and cook 10 minutes more or until vegetables are tender, stirring occasionally. Add chicken, parsley and bacon. Heat through. If desired, garnish with *fresh oregano*.

Serves 4
Prep Time: 15 minutes
Cook Time: 40 minutes

VEGETABLE BEEF SOUP

- 2 cans (10½ ounces *each*) **CAMPBELL'S condensed Beef Broth**
- 2 cups water
- ¼ teaspoon dried thyme leaves, crushed
- ⅛ teaspoon pepper
- 1 medium potato, cut into cubes (about 1 cup)
- 1 bag (16 ounces) frozen mixed vegetables
- ½ cup cut-up canned tomatoes
- 1½ cups cubed cooked beef

- In large saucepan mix broth, water, thyme, pepper, potato, mixed vegetables and tomatoes. Over medium-high heat, heat to a boil. Reduce heat to low. Cover and cook 15 minutes or until vegetables are tender.
- Add beef and heat through.

Serves 4
Prep Time: 15 minutes
Cook Time: 25 minutes

For crispy bacon in a hurry, microwave it. Place bacon on a microwave-safe plate lined with two paper towels. Cover bacon with a paper towel to prevent splattering. One slice of bacon cooks in about 1 minute on HIGH power.

Country Chicken Stew

Dill is a member of the parsley family and is available in three forms: fresh or dried dill weed and dried dill seed.

SEAFOOD CHOWDER

1 tablespoon vegetable oil
1 large onion, chopped (about 1 cup)
⅛ teaspoon garlic powder *or* 1 clove garlic, minced
1 can (10¾ ounces) **CAMPBELL'S** condensed Cream of Celery Soup
1 can (10¾ ounces) **CAMPBELL'S** condensed Cream of Potato Soup
1½ soup cans milk
¼ teaspoon dried dill weed, crushed
½ pound medium shrimp, shelled and deveined
½ pound fresh *or* thawed frozen firm white fish fillets, cut into 1-inch pieces (cod, haddock *or* halibut)

- In large saucepan over medium heat, heat oil. Add onion and garlic powder and cook until tender.
- Add soups, milk and dill. Heat to a boil, stirring often.
- Add shrimp and fish. Cook 5 minutes or until shrimp turn pink and fish flakes easily when tested with a fork, stirring occasionally.

Serves 4
Prep Time: 15 minutes
Cook Time: 20 minutes

Tip: Substitute 2 teaspoons chopped fresh dill for dried and add 2 tablespoons Chablis or other dry white wine with soup.

CHILI CON CARNE

1 pound ground beef
1 medium onion, chopped (about ½ cup)
2 cans (11⅛ ounces *each*) **CAMPBELL'S** condensed Fiesta Tomato Soup
1 cup water
1 can (about 15 ounces) kidney beans, rinsed and drained
Shredded Cheddar cheese

- In medium skillet over medium-high heat, cook beef and onion until beef is browned, stirring to separate meat. Pour off fat.
- Add soup, water and beans. Reduce heat to low and heat through. Garnish with cheese.

Serves 5
Prep Time: 5 minutes
Cook Time: 10 minutes

Seafood Chowder

MEXICAN BEEF STEW

1 ½ pounds ground beef
1 large onion, chopped (about 1 cup)
¼ teaspoon garlic powder *or* 2 cloves garlic, minced
1 can (10¾ ounces) CAMPBELL'S condensed Tomato Soup
1 can (10½ ounces) CAMPBELL'S condensed Beef Broth
1 cup water
2 tablespoons chili powder
3 medium potatoes, cut into cubes (about 3 cups)
1 can (about 16 ounces) whole kernel corn, drained

- In large saucepan over medium-high heat, cook beef, onion and garlic powder until beef is browned, stirring to separate meat. Pour off fat.
- Add soup, broth, water, chili powder and potatoes. Heat to a boil. Reduce heat to low. Cover and cook 15 minutes or until potatoes are tender, stirring occasionally. Add corn. Heat through. Top with shredded *Cheddar cheese*. If desired, garnish with *fresh parsley*.

Serves 6
Prep Time: 15 minutes
Cook Time: 30 minutes

RATATOUILLE SOUP

1 pound ground beef
1 jar (28 ounces) PREGO EXTRA CHUNKY Mushroom & Onion Spaghetti Sauce (3 cups)
1 can (10½ ounces) CAMPBELL'S condensed Beef Broth
2 cups water
1 small eggplant, cut into cubes (about 3½ cups)
1 medium zucchini, cut into cubes (about 1½ cups)
1 large green pepper, chopped (about 1 cup)
½ cup dry elbow macaroni

- In Dutch oven over medium-high heat, cook beef until browned, stirring to separate meat. Pour off fat.
- Add spaghetti sauce, broth, water, eggplant, zucchini and pepper. Heat to boil. Reduce heat to low. Cover and cook 15 minutes, stirring occasionally.
- Stir in macaroni. Reduce heat to medium. Cook 10 minutes or until macaroni is done, stirring occasionally.

Serves 5
Prep Time: 15 minutes
Cook Time: 35 minutes

Mexican Beef Stew

*L*ooking for a casual meal to eat on the run? Try a delicious sandwich or pick-me-up pocket. No utensils required! From contemporary *Chicken Quesadillas* and *Bistro Onion Burgers* to made-for-the 90s *Barbecued Turkey Pockets* and *Tangy Grilled Beef Sandwiches,* these savory sandwiches and burgers will turn a quick lunch into a satisfying meal. Let a can of CAMPBELL'S Soup turn your kitchen into the neighborhood deli — and be ready for mealtime requests time and time again.

Fiesta Tacos, left, (page 141) and Chicken Salad Sandwiches, right, (page 138).

BARBECUED TURKEY POCKETS

    1   can (10 ¾ ounces) **CAMPBELL'S HEALTHY REQUEST** condensed
        Tomato Soup
    ¼   cup water
    2   tablespoons packed brown sugar
    2   tablespoons vinegar
    1   tablespoon Worcestershire sauce
        Thinly sliced cooked turkey breast (about 1 pound)*
    3   pita breads (6-inch), cut in half, forming 2 pockets

- In medium skillet mix soup, water, sugar, vinegar and Worcestershire.
  Over medium heat, heat to a boil. Reduce heat to low and
  cook 5 minutes.
- Add turkey and heat through. Spoon ½ cup turkey mixture into
  each pita half.

Makes 6 sandwiches
Prep Time: 10 minutes
Cook Time: 15 minutes

* (roasted or deli turkey)

CHICKEN SALAD SANDWICHES

    1   can (10 ¾ ounces) **CAMPBELL'S** condensed Cream of Celery Soup
    2   tablespoons mayonnaise
    ¼   teaspoon pepper
    2   cups chopped cooked chicken
    2   stalks celery, sliced (about 1 cup)
    1   small onion, finely chopped (about ¼ cup)
        Lettuce leaves
        Tomato slices
    6   round sandwich rolls, split

- In medium bowl mix soup, mayonnaise and pepper. Stir in chicken,
  celery and onion. Refrigerate at least 4 hours.
- Divide lettuce, tomato and chicken mixture among 6 roll halves.
  Top with remaining roll halves.

Makes 6 sandwiches
Prep Time: 15 minutes
Chill Time: 4 hours

Barbecued Turkey Pockets

*F*or toasted sand-
wich rolls on the
grill, spread cut
sides of rolls with
margarine. Grill
3 to 5 minutes or
until golden.

*T*ANGY GRILLED BEEF SANDWICHES

I	can (10 ¾ ounces) **CAMPBELL'S** condensed Tomato Soup
2	tablespoons packed brown sugar
2	tablespoons lemon juice
2	tablespoons vegetable oil
I	tablespoon Worcestershire sauce
I	teaspoon garlic powder
¼	teaspoon dried thyme leaves, crushed
1½	pounds boneless beef sirloin steak, ¾ inch thick
6	round sandwich rolls, split and toasted

- Mix soup, sugar, lemon juice, oil, Worcestershire, garlic powder and thyme.
- Place steak on lightly oiled grill rack over medium-hot coals. Grill uncovered to desired doneness (allow 15 minutes for medium), turning once and brushing often with soup mixture. Slice steak into thin strips.
- Heat remaining soup mixture to a boil. Divide steak among 6 roll halves. Top with soup mixture and remaining roll halves.

Makes 6 sandwiches
Prep Time: 10 minutes
Cook Time: 15 minutes

FIESTA TACOS

- 1 **pound ground beef**
- 1 **can (11 1/8 ounces) CAMPBELL'S condensed Fiesta Tomato Soup**
- 8 **taco shells**
- 1 **cup shredded lettuce**
- 1 **medium tomato, chopped (about 1 cup)**
- 1 **cup shredded Cheddar cheese (4 ounces)**

- In medium skillet over medium-high heat, cook beef until browned, stirring to separate meat. Pour off fat.
- Add soup. Reduce heat to low and heat through. Divide meat mixture among taco shells. Top with lettuce, tomato and cheese. If desired, garnish with *fresh cherry peppers*.

Makes 8 tacos
Prep Time: 10 minutes
Cook Time: 10 minutes

SOUPERBURGER SANDWICHES

- 1 **pound ground beef**
- 1 **medium onion, chopped (about 1/2 cup)**
- 1 **can (10 3/4 ounces) CAMPBELL'S condensed Cream of Celery Soup**
- 1 **tablespoon prepared mustard**
- 1/8 **teaspoon pepper**
- 6 **hamburger rolls, split and toasted**

- In medium skillet over medium-high heat, cook beef and onion until beef is browned, stirring to separate meat. Pour off fat.
- Add soup, mustard and pepper. Reduce heat to low and heat through. Divide meat mixture among 6 roll halves. Top with remaining roll halves.

Makes 6 sandwiches
Prep Time: 5 minutes
Cook Time: 10 minutes

While cooking the meat mixture, heat the taco shells according to the package directions.

BISTRO ONION BURGERS

1 pouch CAMPBELL'S Dry Onion Soup and Recipe Mix
3 tablespoons water
1½ pounds ground beef
  Lettuce leaves
6 hamburger rolls, split and toasted
  Tomato slices

*S*hape meat
mixture into
patties by hand or
use a patty press.

- Mix soup mix and water. Add beef and mix *thoroughly*. Shape *firmly* into 6 patties, ½ inch thick.
- In medium skillet over medium heat, cook patties in 2 batches 10 minutes or until no longer pink (160°F.), turning once. Set patties aside and keep warm.
- Place lettuce and patties on 6 roll halves. Top with tomato and remaining roll halves.

Makes 6 sandwiches
Prep Time: 10 minutes
Cook Time: 20 minutes

FRENCH DIP SANDWICHES

1 tablespoon cornstarch
1 can (10 ½ ounces) CAMPBELL'S condensed French Onion Soup
½ cup water
8 slices cooked roast beef (about ½ pound)*
4 long hard rolls, split

- In medium skillet mix cornstarch, soup and water. Over medium-high heat, cook until mixture boils and thickens, stirring constantly.
- Add beef. Reduce heat to low and heat through, stirring occasionally. Serve over rolls.

Makes 4 sandwiches
Prep Time: 5 minutes
Cook Time: 10 minutes

* (roasted or deli beef)

*I*TALIAN BURGER MELT

1½ **pounds ground beef**
  1 **can (11⅛ ounces) CAMPBELL'S condensed Italian Tomato Soup**
⅓ **cup water**
  6 **slices mozzarella, process American *or* Monterey Jack cheese
    (about 6 ounces)**
  6 **hamburger rolls, split and toasted**

- Shape beef into 6 patties, ½ inch thick.
- In medium skillet over medium-high heat, cook patties in 2 batches
  until browned. Set patties aside. Pour off fat.
- Add soup and water. Heat to a boil. Return patties to pan.
  Reduce heat to low. Cover and cook 10 minutes or until patties
  are no longer pink (160°F.).
- Place cheese on patties and cook until cheese is melted. Place
  patties on 6 roll halves. Top with soup mixture and remaining
  roll halves.

Makes 6 sandwiches
Prep Time: 10 minutes
Cook Time: 30 minutes

Bistro Onion Burgers
(left), Italian Burger Melt
(right)

CHICKEN FAJITAS

¼ cup prepared Italian salad dressing

6 skinless, boneless chicken breast halves (about 1½ pounds)

1 can (11 ounces) **CAMPBELL'S** condensed Fiesta **Nacho** Cheese Soup

⅓ cup milk

12 flour tortillas (6-inch)

4 green onions, thinly sliced (about ½ cup)

1 small avocado, peeled, pitted and sliced (optional)

- Pour dressing into large shallow nonmetallic dish. Add chicken and turn to coat. Cover and refrigerate 30 minutes, turning chicken occasionally.
- Remove chicken from marinade and place on lightly oiled grill rack over medium-hot coals. Discard marinade. Grill uncovered 15 minutes or until chicken is no longer pink, turning once.
- In small saucepan mix soup and milk. Over medium heat, heat through, stirring often.
- Warm tortillas according to package directions. Slice chicken into thin strips and place down center of each tortilla. Top with onions, avocado and soup mixture. Fold tortilla around filling. If desired, garnish with additional *green onion*.

Makes 12 fajitas

Prep Time: 5 minutes

Marinating Time: 30 minutes

Cook Time: 15 minutes

Tip: Prepare as in first step. In second step remove chicken from marinade and place on rack in broiler pan. Discard marinade. Broil 4 inches from heat 15 minutes or until chicken is no longer pink, turning once. Proceed as in third and fourth steps.

To expedite the ripening process for avocados, place them in a slightly closed paper or plastic bag. Store at room temperature for one to three days.

EEF 'N' BEAN BURRITOS

1 **pound ground beef**
1 **small onion, chopped (about ¼ cup)**
1 **can (11¼ ounces) CAMPBELL'S condensed Fiesta Chili Beef Soup**
¼ **cup water**
8 **flour tortillas (8-inch)**
   Shredded Cheddar cheese
   PACE Thick & Chunky Salsa
   Sour cream (optional)

- In medium skillet over medium-high heat, cook beef and onion until beef is browned, stirring to separate meat. Pour off fat.
- Add soup and water. Reduce heat to low and heat through.
- Warm tortillas according to package directions. Spoon meat mixture down center of each tortilla. Top with cheese, salsa and sour cream. Fold tortilla around filling.

Makes 8 burritos
Prep Time: 10 minutes
Cook Time: 10 minutes

CHICKEN QUESADILLAS

1 **can (10¾ ounces) CAMPBELL'S condensed Cream of Chicken Soup**
1 **jalapeño pepper, seeded and finely chopped (optional)**
1 **cup shredded Cheddar cheese (4 ounces)**
1½ **cups chopped cooked chicken**
8 **flour tortillas (8-inch)**
   PACE Thick & Chunky Salsa
   Sour cream

- In small bowl mix soup, pepper, ½ cup cheese and chicken.
- Place tortillas on 2 large baking sheets. Top half of each tortilla with ¼ cup soup mixture. Spread to within ½ inch of edge. Moisten edges of tortillas with water. Fold over and press edges together.
- Bake at 400°F. for 8 minutes or until hot. Sprinkle with remaining cheese. Serve with salsa and sour cream.

Makes 8 quesadillas
Prep Time: 15 minutes
Cook Time: 8 minutes

When tortillas are warm they are more pliable and easier to roll or fold. See package directions for recommended heating methods.

Beef 'n' Bean Burritos

The secret's in the sauce, many cooks say. And when you're in a rush, the right sauce or topping can make all the difference between ordinary fare and sensational meals. From creamy-rich *Tomato-Basil Pasta Sauce* and shortcut *Cheddar Cheese Sauce* to zesty *Italian Potato Topper* and *Creamy Dijon Dressing,* these and other fabulous recipes provide the perfect solution to a variety of entrées, side dishes and salads. Ready in minutes, these piquant sauces, potato toppers, gravies and salad dressings bring out the best in your family's favorite foods.

Clockwise from top: All-Time Favorite Barbecue Sauce (page 151), Tomato-Basil Pasta Sauce (page 151) and Cheddar Cheese Sauce (page 150).

CHEDDAR CHEESE SAUCE

1 can (10 ¾ ounces) CAMPBELL'S condensed Cheddar Cheese Soup
⅓ cup milk

- In small saucepan mix soup and milk. Over low heat, heat through, stirring often. Serve over French fries, broccoli, cauliflower, carrots, baked potatoes, omelets or pasta.

Makes 1 ½ cups
Prep Time: 5 minutes
Cook Time: 5 minutes

Cheese Sauce Dijonnaise: Add 1 tablespoon Dijon-style mustard.

Cauliflower with Cheddar Cheese Sauce: Add 1 bag (16 ounces) frozen cauliflower, cooked and drained to soup mixture. Heat through.

HERB GRILLING SAUCE

1 can (14 ½ ounces) SWANSON Chicken Broth
3 tablespoons lemon juice
1 teaspoon dried basil leaves, crushed
1 teaspoon dried thyme leaves, crushed
⅛ teaspoon pepper

- Mix broth, lemon juice, basil, thyme and pepper. Use to baste chicken, fish or pork during grilling.

Makes about 2 cups
Prep Time: 10 minutes

Tip: Freeze sauce in ½ cup portions for later use.

Tip: Use sauce as a marinade before grilling.

While vegetables are cooking, use the microwave to heat sauce. In 1-quart microwave-safe bowl, mix soup and milk. Microwave on HIGH 2 ½ minutes or until hot, stirring halfway through heating.

TOMATO-BASIL PASTA SAUCE

- 1 can (10 3/4 ounces) CAMPBELL'S condensed Broccoli Cheese Soup
- 3/4 cup half-and-half *or* milk
- 1 teaspoon dried basil leaves, crushed
- 3 plum tomatoes, coarsely chopped (about 1 cup) *or* 3/4 cup drained cut-up canned plum tomatoes
- 1/4 cup grated Parmesan cheese
- 3 cups hot cooked fettuccine (about 6 ounces dry)

- In medium saucepan mix soup, half-and-half, basil, tomatoes and cheese. Over medium heat, heat to a boil. Reduce heat to low. Cook 5 minutes, stirring occasionally.
- Toss with fettuccine. If desired, garnish with *fresh basil*.

Makes about 2 1/2 cups sauce
Prep Time: 10 minutes
Cook Time: 10 minutes

Tip: Substitute 1 tablespoon chopped fresh basil leaves for dried basil.

ALL-TIME FAVORITE BARBECUE SAUCE

- 1 can (10 3/4 ounces) CAMPBELL'S condensed Tomato Soup
- 1/4 cup vinegar
- 1/4 cup vegetable oil
- 2 tablespoons packed brown sugar
- 1 tablespoon Worcestershire sauce
- 1 teaspoon garlic powder
- 1/8 teaspoon Louisiana-style hot sauce (optional)

- Mix soup, vinegar, oil, sugar, Worcestershire, garlic powder and hot sauce. Use to baste chicken, hamburgers, ribs or steak during broiling or grilling.

Makes 1 1/2 cups
Prep Time: 5 minutes

To chop fresh basil, rinse well and gently pat dry. Discard stems. Chop leaves with an 8-inch chef's knife or place the herb in a 1-cup glass measuring cup and snip it with kitchen scissors.

*B*ROCCOLI CHEESE POTATO TOPPER

1 can (10 ¾ ounces) CAMPBELL'S condensed Cheddar Cheese Soup
2 tablespoons sour cream *or* plain yogurt
½ teaspoon Dijon-style mustard
1 cup cooked broccoli flowerets
4 hot baked potatoes, split

- In medium saucepan mix soup sour cream, mustard and broccoli. Over medium heat, heat through, stirring occasionally.
- Serve over potatoes. If desired, garnish with *red pepper.*

Serves 4
Prep Time: 10 minutes
Cook Time: 10 minutes

Tip: To bake potatoes, pierce with fork. Bake at 400°F. for 1 hour *or* microwave on HIGH 10½ to 12½ minutes or until fork-tender.

*I*TALIAN POTATO TOPPER

1 can (10 ¾ ounces) CAMPBELL'S condensed Cream of Mushroom Soup
Dash pepper
2 cups frozen Italian-style vegetable combination
¼ cup grated Parmesan cheese
4 hot baked potatoes, split
Chopped tomato

- In medium saucepan mix soup, pepper, vegetables and cheese. Over medium heat, heat to a boil.
- Reduce heat to low. Cover and cook 5 minutes or until vegetables are tender, stirring occasionally. Serve over potatoes. Top with tomato.

Serves 4
Prep Time: 5 minutes
Cook Time: 10 minutes

Alternating from top:
Italian Potato Topper,
Broccoli Cheese Potato
Topper

Drippings are the fat and juices given off by meat or poultry as it cooks.

 OUPER GRAVY

- 1 can (10¾ ounces) CAMPBELL'S condensed Cream of Mushroom Soup
- ⅓ cup water
- ¼ cup roasted meat *or* poultry drippings

- Mix soup and water. Add to drippings in roasting pan. Over medium heat, heat through, stirring to loosen browned bits. Serve over roasted meat or poultry.

Makes about 1⅔ cups
Prep Time: 5 minutes
Cook Time: 10 minutes

 EEF GRAVY

- ¼ cup roasted meat drippings
- ¼ cup all-purpose flour
- 1 can (14½ ounces) SWANSON Beef Broth

- In roasting pan or medium saucepan mix drippings and flour. Gradually stir in broth. Over medium heat, cook until mixture boils and thickens, stirring constantly. Serve over roasted meat.

Makes about 2 cups
Prep Time: 5 minutes
Cook Time: 10 minutes

Chicken Gravy: Use poultry drippings for the roasted meat drippings and substitute SWANSON Chicken Broth for the beef broth. Prepare as directed above.

TANGY FRENCH DRESSING

1 **can (10¾ ounces) CAMPBELL'S condensed Tomato Soup**
½ **cup vegetable oil**
¼ **cup vinegar**
½ **teaspoon dry mustard**

- In small bowl or jar mix soup, oil, vinegar and mustard. Refrigerate at least 2 hours. Stir or shake before serving.

Makes 2 cups
Prep Time: 5 minutes
Chill Time: 2 hours

Tip: Substitute CAMPBELL'S HEALTHY REQUEST Tomato Soup for tomato soup.

CREAMY DIJON DRESSING

1 **can (10¾ ounces) CAMPBELL'S HEALTHY REQUEST condensed Cream of Celery Soup**
½ **cup mayonnaise**
¼ **cup water**
2 **tablespoons vinegar**
2 **tablespoons Dijon-style mustard**
½ **teaspoon garlic powder**

- In small bowl mix soup, mayonnaise, water, vinegar, mustard and garlic powder. Refrigerate at least 2 hours. Stir before serving.

Makes 2 cups
Prep Time: 5 minutes
Chill Time: 2 hours

---

*V*inegars are most commonly derived from grapes (wine vinegar) or apples (cider vinegar) or grains (white or distilled vinegar). Keep vinegar tightly capped and store on the pantry shelf for six months.

INDEX

PRODUCT INDEX